Stylish Knits for Dogs

QUARRY

BEVERLY MASSACHUSETTS

QUARRY BOOKS

Stylish Knits for Dogs

36 Projects to Knit in a Weekend

Ilene Hochberg

First published in the United States of America by

Quarry Books, a member of

Quayside Publishing Group

100 Cummings Center

Suite 406-L

Beverly, Massachusetts 01915-6101

Telephone: (978) 282-9590

Fax: (978) 283-2742

www.quarrybooks.com

Library of Congress Cataloging-in-Publication Data

Hochberg, Ilene, 1955–

  Stylish knits for dogs : 36 projects to knit in a weekend / Ilene Hochberg.

    p. cm.

  ISBN 1-59253-214-4 (paperback)

  1. Knitting—Patterns. 2. Dogs—Equipment and supplies. 3. Sweaters. I. Title.

  TT825.H54 2006

  746.43'20432—dc22   2005023446

                                               CIP

ISBN 1-59253-214-4

10 9 8 7 6 5

Design: Dania Davey

Production Design: Laura H. Couallier, Laura Herrmann Design

Cover Design: Sniff Design Studio

Photography: Rob Upton

Printed in Singapore

Dedication

To Irwin Hochberg, who always believed in
me, and to Bob Wood, who believes in me now

For all the dogs in my heart:
Nubie,
Tori,
Morgan,
Annabel,
Bubbles,
Suds,
Bucky,
Chloe,
Charlie,
Susannah,
Sassy,
Kelly,
Beanie,
Brandy,
and Brownie,
who started it all

Contents

Introduction

If you are anything like me, you have bought this book for two reasons. You love your dog, and you love to knit. Those were my reasons for writing *Stylish Knits for Dogs: 36 Projects to Knit in a Weekend.*

I've been involved with pets and fashion since 1984 when I started a company called Dogwear that designed and distributed functional fashions for pets. I produced a press piece called *Dogwear Daily*, which looked just like *Women's Wear Daily*, the fashion newspaper. My version featured dogs wearing sweaters, T-shirts, collars, and leashes of my design. The newsletter proved so popular that I expanded it into what I thought would be a once-off version of a pet fashion magazine. I called my book *Dogue* (named after *Vogue*, naturally).

Dogue was an instant success, and jumped to the top of bestseller lists across the country and abroad. I appeared on television (*Good Morning America, CNN,* and local news shows everywhere), and was interviewed by more magazines and newspapers than I can name. Suddenly I was perceived as a leading authority on pet fashions and the many ways to pamper your four-legged friends!

knit to relax

As I traveled around the country to promote the book, knitting kept me calm and grounded. I knit in airports before my flights; in cars on the way to interviews; and even in bookstores, while I waited to autograph copies of my book. I made dozens of sweaters for my own dogs, and visited knitting stores in every major city to replenish my yarn supplies.

Upon my return home, I submitted dog sweater designs to the major knitting magazines, and my designs were selected for publication. I decided to close Dogwear so that I would have more time to write new books, and to knit.

To date, I have published five magazine parodies (*Dogue, Catmopolitan, Vanity Fur, Forbabes,* and *Good Mousekeeping*) and the parody of a popular business book (*Who Stole My Cheese?!!*). *Stylish Knits for Dogs* will be my seventh book and marks my return to the subject I know and love best—designer sweaters for dogs.

simple and stylish

Most of the designs found in this book are easy enough for new knitters. A simple dog sweater can be finished in less time than it takes to make the scarves that beginning knitters typically choose as their first projects. Depending upon the size of your dog, a sweater can be completed in just a couple of hours, and will certainly be done by the time the late-night comedians go off the air for the night. How's that for instant gratification?

Most of the sweater designs in this book are composed of two simple pieces: a rectangle that forms the back of the sweater and a triangle that covers the chest. The cardigan designs, which, like the people versions, button down the front, are made from five easy pieces, which include the back, two fronts, and two sleeves. These designs are slightly more complicated than the pullover patterns and should be tackled by more experienced knitters, as they require a bit more shaping and sewing.

finding a custom fit

Each of the sweater designs can be made in a range of sizes to fit most types of small to medium dogs, from tiny toy breeds that can be held in the palm of your hand (size 8) to the medium size breeds, such as terriers and spaniels (size 18). Larger dogs do not typically wear sweaters, but if you wish to dress a Great Dane or Saint Bernard, you can adapt these patterns proportionately to accommodate giant breeds. Instructions are given on how to measure your pet to achieve a sweater that will fit correctly (see sizing guidelines, page 23).

Most of the designs are made with worsted-weight yarn, or can be knit using two strands of sport-weight yarn held together. A couple of the designs use chunky-weight yarn, which knits up in a flash. Be certain to knit a swatch to check your gauge (the number of stitches per inch or centimeter) to be certain that your sweater will fit your dog when you are through.

matching yarns to projects

A specific yarn will be recommended for each sweater design. This is the yarn used to knit the sample sweater and will result in a sweater identical to the one photographed. You can purchase these yarns at your local yarn store, or online, directly from the manufacturer. You can substitute another yarn for the ones recommended, but be certain to knit up a gauge swatch (see page 21), to be sure that your yarn choice will produce the gauge required to knit a sweater that will fit your pet.

I recommend that you use synthetic (acrylic or nylon blends) or superwash wool yarns so the sweaters can be easily washed in a machine. (Dogs tend to get dirty, and so do their sweaters!) You may also use specialized, more luxurious yarns, such as cashmere, or wools that have not been specially treated for ease of care, but these will require hand washing in cold water to ensure that they will not shrink or felt. Save these yarns for splurge items and special-occasion ensembles.

people sweaters

You can look as stylish as your dog! I have provided instructions for "people" versions or adaptations of some sweaters (see pages 42, 50, 54, 102, 114, and 116). Mother-doggie fashions ... People- and pet-coordinated designs ... Who ever thought that dressing like your dog could be so fashionable and so fun! Bow *Wow!*

knitting basics

You need to acquire four foundation techniques when you are learning to knit: **casting on**, **knitting**, **purling**, and **binding off**. Everything else is a variation on these basics. A simplified presentation of these techniques follows.

BASIC STITCHES

Casting On

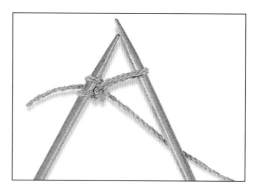

Fig 1.0: **Casting on** creates a row of loops on one knitting needle to form the base row for the knitting. All cast-on methods begin with a slipknot. To form the slip-knot for the first stitch, make a pretzel-shaped loop with the yarn; insert one needle under one length and draw through the loop and tighten. One cast-on method is the cable cast-on, which is shown here.

Form a slipknot about 10" (25 cm) away from the end of the yarn. Place the slipknot on one knitting needle and tighten the knot around the needle. Hold this needle in your left hand. Hold the other needle in your right hand. Insert the right needle from underneath into the loop on the left-hand needle, starting at the base in the front and ending in the back of the left-hand needle. From the back, wrap the working yarn (the strand attached to the ball) around the right needle and pull the yarn through the center of the loop on the needle, forming another loop. Transfer this loop up and over the tip of the left needle, making two stitches that are next to each other.

Fig 1.1: For the next cast-on stitch, insert the right needle tip from the near side to the far side between the first two stitches on the left needle. From the back, wrap the working yarn around the right needle and draw the new stitch through the middle of the two stitches. Pull it up and over the point of the left needle in the same manner for this third stitch. Continue in this manner, inserting in between the last two stitches on the needle, until you have cast on the desired number of stitches.

The Knit Stitch

Fig 2.0: Once you have cast on, you will then knit into these stitches to form the knitted fabric. Hold the needle with the stitches in your left hand with the first stitch near the point of the needle. Hold the empty needle in your right hand. Insert the right needle from front to back into the first stitch on the left needle, keeping the right needle under the left needle and the yarn at the back. Bring the working yarn (the strand attached to the ball) clockwise over the right needle as shown in the photo and pull it gently between the two needles. Use your right index finger as necessary to guide the yarn.

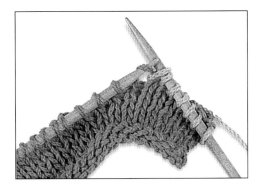

Fig 2.1: With the point of the right needle, catch the yarn and pull it through the stitch on the left needle. Slip the old stitch off the left needle, leaving the new stitch on the right needle. Repeat these steps until all the stitches have been knit onto the right needle to complete a row of knitting.

The Purl Stitch

Fig 3.0: **The purl stitch** is the reverse of the knit stitch. Hold the needle with the stitches in your left hand and the empty needle in your right hand. In the case of the purl stitch, the working yarn (the strand attached to the ball) is held to the front of the work. Insert the right needle from back to front into the first stitch. The right needle is in front of the left needle, and the yarn is in front of the needles. Wrap the yarn counterclockwise around the right needle as shown.

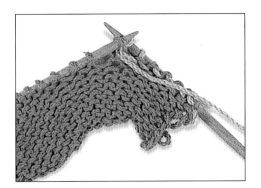

Fig 3.1: With the point of the right needle, catch the yarn and draw it backward through the stitch on the left needle, forming a loop on the right needle. Slip this stitch off the left needle, leaving the new stitch on the right needle. Repeat these steps until all the stitches on the left needle have been knit onto the right needle to complete a row of purling.

Stockinette stitch is a basic pattern in knitting. One row of stitches is knit and the next row is purled, and these two rows are repeated to create this common fabric.

BASIC STITCHES

Binding Off

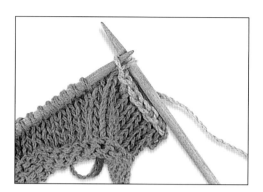

Fig 4.0: This is the technique used to finish the knitted fabric to prevent it from unraveling. To start, knit the first two stitches. Insert the point of the left-hand needle into the first stitch on the right needle. Pull this stitch over the second stitch and off the right-hand needle. Knit the next stitch on the left-hand needle so that there are two stitches on the right-hand needle again. Insert the point of the left-hand needle into the first stitch on the right-hand needle.

Fig 4.1: Pull this stitch over the second stitch and off the right-hand needle. Continue in this manner until all the stitches have been bound off, leaving one stitch left on the needle. Clip the yarn, leaving a tail, and thread the yarn through this last stitch and pull to fasten it off.

GLOSSARY—CAST-ON Techniques

Backward Loop Cast On

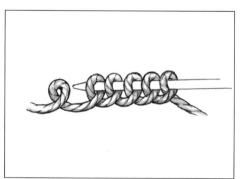

Cable Cast On

* Make a backward loop as shown and place it on the needle in a backward position so that it doesn't unwind. Repeat from * as necessary.

Step 1: Form a slipknot with a 10" (25 cm) tail. Place the knot on a knitting needle and cinch it. Hold this needle in your left hand. Slip the other needle from underneath into the loop, starting at the base in the front and ending in the back of the left-hand needle. From the back, wrap the working yarn around the right needle and pull the yarn through the center of the loop on the needle, forming another loop. Transfer this loop onto the tip of the left needle, making two stitches that are next to each other. For the next cast-on stitch, insert the right needle tip from the near side to the far side between the first two stitches on the left needle.

(continued)

Cable Cast On (cont.)

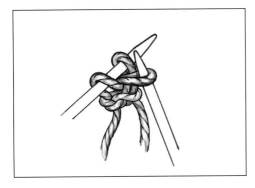

Step 2: From the back, wrap the working yarn around the tip of the right needle and draw the new stitch through the middle of the two stitches.

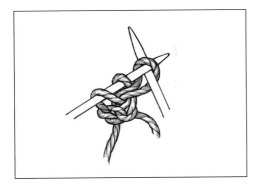

Step 3: Pull this stitch up and over the point of the left needle in the same manner for this third stitch. Continue in this manner, inserting in between the last two stitches on the needle, until you have cast on the desired number of stitches.

Crochet Chain Provisional Cast On

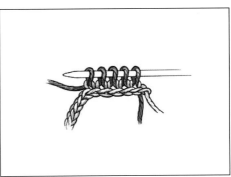

Step 1: With crochet hook and a length of smooth waste cotton yarn, make a crochet chain 2–4 stitches longer than the number of stitches required for cast on. Using the needle and yarn specified in the pattern instructions, pick up the back loop of the chain stitch and knit a stitch.

Step 2: Later, following knitting instructions, pull out waste yarn to expose live stitches; place live stitches on knitting needle and work as directed.

CAST-ON Techniques

Single Crochet

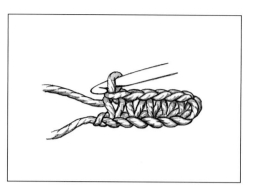

Step 1: Make a slipknot and place it on hook. *Bring the yarn over hook as shown and draw it through the slipknot. Repeat from * as necessary. To complete crochet chain, cut yarn and bring yarn tail through last loop on the crochet hook; pull yarn tail to tighten and secure.

Step 3: Draw it through both loops on hook.

Step 2: Insert the hook into a stitch, wrap the yarn over the hook, and draw a loop through stitch; wrap the yarn over the hook.

One-Row Buttonhole

The bottom edge of the buttonhole is worked on the right side of the fabric and the top edge is worked on the wrong side of the fabric, all within the same row. Work to the point where the instructions specify to begin buttonholes. Bring the yarn between the needle tips to the front of the work. Slip the next stitch purlwise, then take the yarn between the needle tips to the back of the work and leave it there.

Step 1: *Slip next stitch from left needle to right needle. Then, on right needle, pass second stitch over end stitch and drop it off needle (one stitch bound off). Repeat from * the number of times required to bind off the buttonhole stitches specified in pattern. Return last slipped stitch to left needle and turn the work.

Step 2: With yarn in back and using the cable cast-on method, cast on one more stitch than was bound off. Turn the work.

Step 3: With yarn in back, slip first stitch from left needle to right needle, then pass the extra cable cast-on stitch over it to close buttonhole. Adjust the stitches and tighten as necessary. Work across row to next buttonhole position and repeat as above.

FINISHING Techniques

Felting

Anyone who has accidentally run a wool sweater through a hot-water wash has felted a project, though the results were not planned. Felting creates a dense, fuzzy finish to wool knits. It can be functional (adding warmth to mittens or slippers) or decorative (altering the shape and "look" of a handbag).

Weave in all loose yarn tails to wrong side of work. Partially fill a washing machine with hot water. Add a small amount of mild detergent or dishwashing liquid (too many suds will hamper the felting process). Place the item to be felted in an enclosed pillowcase. Use a separate pillowcase for smaller pieces, such as straps, pockets, and so on, to avoid tangles. Place the pillow-case(s) in washer. (You may add a heavy pair of jeans, or sneakers, to the wash, to increase agitation and aid in the felting process. Note: If your yarn is not colorfast, other items may be discolored in the process.) Set the washing machine at its longest wash cycle.

Check the felting process frequently (every five minutes). Monitoring the process is crucial, as it difficult to stretch and reshape a project that has shrunken too small. Reset wash cycle as needed until all items are felted satisfactorily. Felting usually takes several repetitions of the hot-water agitation steps. Felting is complete when the stitches are obscured and the fabric is firm. Turn to spin cycle and remove excess water. Stretch bags and hats over suitable forms to shape. Felted items should fit forms snugly. Mold, pull, and poke the fabric until desired shape or size is obtained. Hang straps to dry. Allow to completely air dry. Keep in mind when planning a felting project that superwash wools and synthetic yarns will not felt.

Hand Felting

To felt small items by hand, fill a dishpan or sink with hot water, add a small amount of dishwashing soap, and vigorously rub all parts of item until fabric becomes dense and it is difficult or impossible to see individual stitches. Rinse well several times to remove any soapy residue. Shape item and allow it to air dry.

Kitchener Stitch (Grafting)

This technique is useful for creating an invisible seam between rows of live stitches, maintaining a fabric's smooth weave. Don't work grafted stitches too tightly. It's easier to tighten them later, if necessary.

Step 1: Bring threaded tapestry needle through first front stitch purlwise and leave stitch on needle.

Step 2: Bring threaded tapestry needle through first back stitch knitwise and leave stitch on needle.

Step 3: Bring threaded tapestry needle through same front stitch knitwise and slip stitch off needle.

Step 4: Bring threaded tapestry needle through next front stitch purlwise and leave stitch on needle.

Step 5: Bring threaded tapestry needle through first back stitch purlwise and slip stitch off needle.

Step 6: Bring threaded tapestry needle through next back stitch knitwise and leave stitch on needle.

Step 7: Keeping the work loose, repeat steps 3 through 6 until no stitches remain on needles.

Step 8: With tapestry needle, gently arrange grafted stitches so that they match the knitting tension.

CAST-ON Techniques

Three-Needle Bind Off

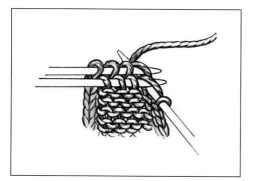

The three-needle bind off is a useful technique to join stitches head to head. You do two things at once: bind off and join two pieces together, which is great for joining shoulder seams. To do the three-needle bind off, you need three needles in the appropriate size for your project: one each to hold the shoulder stitches and one for working the actual bind off.

Place each set of shoulder stitches onto a separate needle. (The needles holding these stitches may be smaller in size than those previously used.) With right sides of work facing together, needles parallel, and tips pointing in same direction, *insert a third needle (of the same size as used in pattern) into first stitch on front needle and into first stitch on back needle. Knit both stitches together (one stitch on third needle); repeat once (two stitches on third needle), then pass first stitch over second stitch, as with a normal bind off. Repeat from * until just one stitch remains on third needle. Fasten off by cutting the yarn, leaving a 6" (15 cm) tail, and pulling tail through last stitch to secure it.

I-CORD Techniques

I-Cord

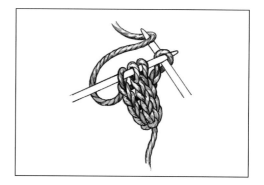

With double-pointed needles, cast on number of stitches specified in pattern. *Without turning needle, slide stitches to other end of needle, pull yarn around back to needle tip, and knit the stitches as usual; repeat from * for required length.

Attached I-Cord: Working I-cord described previously and using a stitch pickup ratio as indicated in your pattern, *knit 2 stitches (or the number of I-cord stitches specified), slip garment-edge stitch onto right needle knitwise, then work an ssk (see Abbreviations, page 22) using last stitch of I-cord row with first picked-up stitch in garment edge. Slip I-cord stitches to other end of double-pointed needles, pull working yarn from around back to needle tip, and work from *.

Alternate I-Cord Method: This method was introduced to knitters by Joyce Williams. It's suitable to use when working the I-cord in one color and the garment or item in another color. Work I-cord (see above) over specified number of stitches, *knit to last I-cord stitch, slip it knitwise onto right needle, yarn over, insert tip of right-hand needle into picked-up edge stitch and knit 1, then pass both the yarn over and last I-cord stitch over. Slide I-cord stitches to end of double-pointed needles, pull working yarn from around back to needle tip, and work from *.

I-Cord Bind Off–
Circular Method

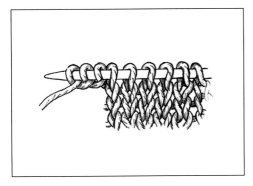

Step 1: With right side of work facing, cast on specified number of stitches for pattern onto right-hand tip of circular needle using backward loop cast on (see page 16). These stitches form the I-cord tail through last stitch to secure it.

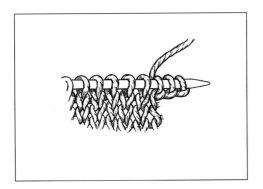

Step 2: Slip these cast-on I-cord stitches from right needle to left needle (working yarn will be away from needle tip by the same number of I-cord stitches slipped onto left needle). *Pull the yarn behind the cast-on stitches to front of needle tip, knit to last I-cord stitch.

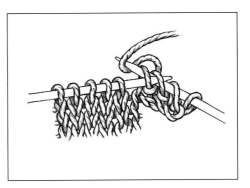

Step 3: Then knit into back loop of both the last I-cord stitch and the first edge stitch at the same time (one stitch is bound off). Return I-cord stitches to left needle *.

GAUGE

The knitting gauge is the number of stitches and rows per inch (or centimeter). It determines the size your finished piece will be. It is critical that you follow the gauge in knitting patterns. Everyone knits differently; some people knit tightly, some loosely, and some in the middle. Before you begin the item, you need to knit a swatch in the pattern stitch using the yarn you have chosen for the project. This simple swatch can save you from creating something that is the wrong size. The test swatch must be at least 4" (10 cm) square. Measure your swatch using a ruler or knit gauge tool. If the number of stitches and rows does not match the gauge specified in the pattern, you need to change the needle size. To get more stitches per unit of measure, use a smaller needle size; to get fewer stitches per unit of measure, use a larger needle size.

ABBREVIATIONS

Knitting has its own language. The following is a list of common knitting abbreviations used in the patterns in this book.

beg—begin; beginning; begins

bet—between

BO—bind off; binding off; bound off

CC—contrast color(s)

ch—chain, as in crochet

cm—centimeter(s)

cn—cable needle

CO—cast on; casting on

cont—continue; continuing; continued

dec(s)—decrease(s); decreasing; decreased

dpn—double-pointed needle(s)

foll—follow; following

fwd—forward

g—gram(s)

inc—increase(s); increasing; increased

k—knit

k1f&b—knit into the front and then the back loop of same stitch

k2tog—knit two stitches together

kwise—knitwise (as if to knit)

m(s)—marker(s)

MC—main color

mm—millimeter(s)

M1—make one stitch (increase). Insert the left needle under the horizontal strand between the stitch on the left needle and the one just worked, forming a loop on the left needle; then, with the right needle, knit into the front strand of the loop, thereby twisting the stitch and closing any hole.

M1L—make one left. With left needle tip, lift strand between needles from front to back. Knit lifted loop through the back.

M1R—make one right. With left needle tip, lift strand between needles from back to front. Knit lifted loop through the front.

p—purl

p1f&b—purl into front and back of same stitch

p2tog—purl two stitches together

patt(s)—pattern(s)

pm—place marker

psso—pass slipped stitch over

pwise—purlwise (as if to purl)

rem—remain; remaining; remainder

rep—repeat(s); repeating; repeated

rev St st—reverse stockinette stitch (purl side of work is used as the right side)

rib—ribbing

rnd(s)—round(s), as in circular knitting

RS—right side

rev sc—reverse single crochet

sc—single crochet

sk—skip

sl—slip

sl st—slip stitch

ssk—slip 2 stitches knitwise, one at a time, from the left needle to the right needle. Insert the left needle tip into the fronts of both slipped stitches and knit them together from this position.

st(s)—stitch(es)

St st—stockinette stitch

tbl—through the back loop of a stitch

tog—together

WS—wrong side

wyb—with yarn in back of work

wyf—with yarn in front of work

yo—yarn over

SIZE SPECIFICATIONS

The sweaters in this book are made in sizes Small, Medium, and Large.

Size Small will fit most puppies and small dogs, such as the toy breeds. Toy breeds include the Chihuahua, Italian Greyhound, Maltese, Manchester Toy Terrier, Miniature Pinscher, Papillion, Pekingese, Pomeranian, Toy Poodle, Pug, Shih Tsu, Silky Terrier, and Yorkshire Terrier, among others. Another way to measure your dog is by weight. Size Small will fit dogs that weigh less than ten pounds (4.5 kg).

Size Medium will fit medium-size dogs, such as the Miniature Dachshund, smaller terriers, which include the Australian Terrier, Border Terrier, Cairn Terrier, Lakeland Terrier, Miniature Schnauzer, Norfolk Terrier, Norwich Terrier, Scottish Terrier, and the West Highland White Terrier, as well as the Cocker Spaniel, Bichon Frise, Lhasa Apso, and Miniature Poodle. Size Medium will fit dogs that weigh from twelve to twenty pounds (5.5–9 kg). Some dogs of the breeds mentioned above may exceed this weight guideline. In these cases, knit a size Large sweater.

Size Large will fit large size dogs such as the Beagle, Basset Hound, Shetland Sheepdog, Welsh Corgi, Dachshund, Bull Terrier, Fox Terrier, Irish Terrier, Kerry Blue Terrier, Manchester Terrier, Soft-Coated Wheaten Terrier, and the Bulldog. Size Large will fit dogs that weigh from twenty-five to forty pounds (11.5–18 kg).

Another way to determine the right size for your dog is to measure around the largest part of his chest ("circumference" in each sweater size specification) and down the back from the base of his neck (where the collar would go), to the base of his tail ("back length" in each sweater specification). Compare these measurements to the size specifications given for each sweater to find the best fit for your pet.

How to Put On a Dog Sweater

Okay, stop laughing. You know that I mean how to put a dog sweater onto your dog. Size Small, Medium, and Large will fit your pet a lot better than they will fit you.

If you have never dressed your dog in a sweater, you are both in for a fun experience—really! The first thing to do is to knit a dog sweater in the right size to fit your pet. That done, hold the sweater in your hands and starting at the bottom end, gather it up to the neck, much like you would do with a knee sock or pair of stockings.

Next, grab a hold of your pet, and gently ease the sweater over his head, stretching the neck opening large enough to permit his head to pop through with a minimum of struggling. Now, reach your hand into one of the leg openings from the outside, and firmly grasp your pet's corresponding front leg within the sweater. It may be helpful to cup your hand over his paw so that his toenails will not catch in your handiwork as you ease his leg out of the "sleeve." Repeat this process on the other side of the sweater with his other front leg.

Finally, pull the bottom of the sweater down the length of his body so that the hem sits at the base of his tail, and smooth the sweater into place.

Voila—another supermodel is born!

Chapter One

knit togs for dogs

knit togs for dogs

Knitting dog sweaters can be a rewarding experience. They are fun to make, quick to complete, and will fit your dog without restricting movement. I call my designs **"functional fashions for pets"** because they will protect your dog from the cold, while providing your favorite four-legged friend with a unique sense of style. Don't you wish that all your knitting projects could be this satisfying and easy?

basic turtleneck sweater

This pattern is the simplest one in the book, and it provides you with the most design versatility. Knit it as written to produce a plain, solid-color turtleneck sweater, or choose washable synthetic fiber yarns, washable wool yarns, or more precious fibers such as alpaca or cashmere for special occasions. Embellish this basic pattern with sewn-on details, such as buttons, bows, or beads to create a one-of-a-kind design.

INSTRUCTIONS FOR
BASIC TURTLENECK SWEATER

BACK

▶ Starting at hem edge, cast on 36 (48, 56) sts. Work in 2 × 2 rib (k2, p2 every row) for 2 (2, 3)" (5 [5, 8] cm) to form ribbing at hem.

▶ Change to St st for 8 (12, 17)" (20 [30, 43] cm) to form body of sweater. Change back to 2 × 2 rib and work for 4" (10 cm) to create turtleneck of sweater.

▶ Bind off in rib stitch, leaving a length of yarn attached to be used to sew together the sweater.

CHEST

▶ Starting at hem edge, cast on 20 (24, 32) sts. Work in 2 × 2 rib for 2 (2, 3)" (5 [5, 8] cm) to form ribbing at hem.

▶ Change to St st for 1 (2, 3)" (3 [5, 8] cm). Continue in St st, decreasing 1 st (k2tog) at beg and end of all following knit rows until 1 st remains on the needle.

▶ Cut and pull yarn through remaining loop to fasten at point of triangle, leaving a length of yarn attached to be used to sew together the sweater.

Finishing

Starting at the turtleneck end of the back, use the attached length of yarn to sew together the ribbed portion to form the neck of the sweater. Use a yarn needle that has an eye large enough to accommodate the yarn but a blunt tip to prevent shredding to sew the sweater together. Do not cut the loose end of yarn when you are done. This will be used to sew the chest to the back of the sweater.

Fit the triangular portion of the chest piece under this turtleneck (there is a "top" of the triangle at the end opposite the cast-on edge; this "top" will be identified by the attached length of yarn at this point) and use the remaining yarn to sew one side of the triangular form to the adjoining stockinette stitch portion of the back piece. Fasten yarn here securely and conceal end by pulling the needle through a few stitches at the reverse side of the garment. Cut yarn.

Use the length of yarn at the top of the triangle to sew the other triangular portion of the chest to the back. Conceal the end of yarn as described above and cut off. Thread a length of matching yarn through your needle and sew the ribbed portion of the chest piece to the adjoining sides of the back piece, making the chest piece lie flat against the back portion of the sweater. This will leave two openings, one at each side, to accommodate the dog's legs (armholes).

If you wish, you may use a crochet hook to attach a new length of yarn ½" (1 cm) from the center of the hem. Chain a length about 1" (3 cm) long and attach other end at the point ½" (1 cm) from the center on the other side. This will create a loop through which you can pull the dog's tail to secure the sweater to your pet at the hem of the garment. Weave in any loose ends with yarn needle.

MATERIALS

1 skein worsted-weight yarn, Kraemer Yarns Summit Hill (100% merino superwash wool; 3.5 oz [100 g]/230 yd [210 m]) in desired color

US size 9 (5.5 mm) straight needles or size to obtain gauge

Yarn needle

Crochet hook (optional)

Finished Dimensions

Directions are for sizes small (medium, large).

Back: length 10 (14, 20)" (25 [36, 51] cm), 4" (10 cm) turtleneck, width 9 (12, 14)" (23 [30, 36] cm)

Chest: width 5 (6, 8)" (13 [15, 20] cm)

Circumference: 14 (18, 22)" (36 [46, 56] cm)

Gauge: 4 sts and 6 rows = 1" (3 cm) in stockinette stitch

4" × 4" (10 × 10 cm) swatch = 16 sts and 24 rows

embellished variations

dog bone sweater

Hand-crocheted dog bones are easy and fun to make, even if you have never crocheted before. Make one or more in each of the four sizes, and sew them onto a turtleneck sweater for an unexpected accent to basic black.

INSTRUCTIONS FOR
CROCHETED DOG BONES

▶ Make slipknot near end of yarn. Place knot onto crochet hook. This is the first stitch. Chain 7 (9, 11, 13) and turn work.

▶ Single crochet in each stitch, skipping the first chain for the turn, 7 (9, 11, 13) stitches. Chain one to turn and work a single crochet into each stitch on the other side of the foundation chain, 7 (9, 11, 13) stitches. Complete a slip stitch at the end of the row.

▶ Work 4 double-crochet stitches into the last stitch in the row, next to the slip stitch. Make a slip stitch into the stitch. Work 4 double-crochet stitches next to the new slip stitch on the other side of the same stitch. Make a slip stitch into the same stitch.

1 skein worsted-weight
    yarn, Kraemer Yarns
    Summit Hill (100%
    merino superwash wool;
    3.5 oz [100 g]/230 yd
    [210 m]) in pearl or
    desired color

Crochet hook size J or 9

Yarn needle to sew bones
    onto sweater

Finished Dimensions

Directions are for sizes
    small (medium, large,
    extra large).

Length: $2\frac{1}{2}$ (3, $3\frac{1}{2}$, 4)"
    (6 [8, 9, 10] cm)

▶ Pull yarn through to back of work and cut off. Leave a length of yarn three times as long as the perimeter measurement of the bone. This yarn will be used to sew the bone onto the sweater.

▶ At the other end of 3-row foundation chain, attach a new length of yarn by doing a slip stitch into the last stitch in the row. Work 4 double-crochet stitches into the same stitch. Make a slip stitch into the same stitch. Work 4 double-crochet stitches next to the new slip stitch on the other side of the same stitch. Make a slip stitch into the same stitch.

▶ Pull yarn through to back of work and cut off, leaving a length of yarn three times as long as the perimeter of the bone attached to the work that will be used to sew the bone to the sweater.

▶ Make one bone in each of the four sizes, or make more if you wish to embellish a larger-sized sweater. Sew these bones onto the back of the sweater in an arrangement of your choice.

embellished variations

pearls turtleneck sweater

Pearls are, of course, the sophisticated choice for day or evening. Stitch an assortment onto a black Basic Turtleneck Sweater (see page 28) for a classic nighttime look or onto a rose-colored sweater, as shown here, for a feminine daytime fashion. You can also sew pearls around the neck of a crewneck sweater for a vintage choker effect.

pocket sweater

This clever little pocket is the ideal place to stash a bone or some biscuits. The button will keep your dog's treasures secure! This design can be knit in a solid color or in muted tones for a quieter appearance. Although shown here on the Basic Turtleneck Sweater (see page 28), it would make a great embellishment to any of the sweater patterns in this book.

INSTRUCTIONS FOR
POCKET SWEATER

POCKET

Cast on 12 sts. Knit in St st until square (until piece measures 4" [10 cm]). Bind off.

POCKET FLAP

▶ Cast on 12 sts. Work in St st for four rows.

▶ Next row, continue in St st, but decrease 1 st (k2tog) at beg and end of all following knit rows until 1 st remains.

▶ Cut yarn and pull through loop. Weave in remaining tail to wrong side of flap.

Finishing

Center the pocket on the back of sweater and sew into place. Sew button to pocket under point of flap and pull button through a stitch in the point of the flap (a makeshift buttonhole) to reveal button.

ADDITIONAL MATERIALS

- One-eighth skein bulky weight yarn, Kraemer Yarns Mauch Chunky (100% wool; 3.5 oz [100 g]/120 yd [110 m]) in pumpkin or desired color

- US size 11 (5.5 mm) straight needles or size to obtain gauge

- Purchased button in desired color, 1" (3 cm) purple shown here

- Yarn needle to sew pocket onto sweater

Gauge: 3 sts and 4 rows = 1" (3 cm) in stockinette stitch

4" × 4" (10 × 10 cm) swatch = 12 sts and 16 rows

pom-pom sweater

Pom-poms add color and whimsy to the Basic Turtleneck Sweater (see page 28). This sweater is a cinch to make. Simply knit the Basic Turtleneck Sweater pattern in your favorite color (red is shown here, but it looks elegant in black), and sew on pom-poms for a lighthearted and multidimensional effect.

crystals turtleneck sweater

Create dazzling evening attire for your pet by sewing clear, plastic "crystals" onto the Basic Turtleneck Sweater (see page 28), as shown here in black. Or, stitch crystals onto a pastel or cream-colored sweater for a delicate, dressy look. (You can find crystals in most craft stores.)

v-neck sweater

Here is another basic design ready for you to customize for your pet. It is shown with contrasting neck and bottom banding, but you can also knit it in solids, stripes, textures, or with any of the novelty yarns that change color and texture all on their own.

INSTRUCTIONS FOR V-NECK SWEATER

BACK

Using CC and starting at hem edge, cast on 26 (34, 42) sts. Work as follows for 1" (3 cm):

Row 1 (RS): *K2, p2, rep from * across row, k2.

Row 2 (WS): *P2, k2, rep from * across row, p2.

Change to MC and work in St st until piece measures 10 (14, 20)" (25 [36, 51] cm) to form body of sweater, ending in a purl row. Next row: using CC, work as follows for 1" (3 cm) to form back of v-neck of sweater:

Row 1 (RS): *K2, p2, rep from * across row, k2.

Row 2 (WS): *P2, k2, rep from * across row, p2.

Bind off in rib pattern, leaving a length of yarn to be used to sew together the sweater.

CHEST

Using CC, cast on 16 (18, 24) sts. For sizes small and large, work in 2 x 2 rib (k2, p2 every row) for 1" (3 cm). For size medium, work as follows for 1" (3 cm):

Row 1 (RS): *K2, p2, rep from * across row, k2.

Row 2 (WS): *P2, k2, rep from * across row, p2.

Change to MC and work in St st for 2 (3, 5)" (5 [8, 13] cm). For next few rows, follow instructions as follows:

Next row (RS): K2tog at beg of row and k4 (5, 8) sts. K2tog. Attach a new ball of yarn and k2tog. This will form the bottom of the v-neck. K4 (5, 8) sts. K2tog.

Next row (WS): Purl.

***Next row (RS):** K2tog, knit until 2 sts remain on this side of neckline. K2tog. Repeat this on the other side of the neckline, decreasing from both sides of the neckline on the knit rows.

WS: Purl.*

Repeat these two rows (from * to *) until 1 st remains on needle on each side of neckline. Pull end of yarn through each of these stitches to fasten off work at points of triangles. Cut off remaining yarn, leaving a length attached to chest plate to be used to sew together the chest of the sweater.

MATERIALS

1 skein main color (MC) and 1 skein contrast color (CC) bulky weight yarn, Kraemer Yarns Mauch Chunky (100% wool; 3.5 oz [100 g]/120 yd [110 m]) in almond (MC) and plum (CC) or desired colors

US size 11 (8 mm) straight needles or size to obtain gauge

Size K crochet hook

Yarn needle

Finished Dimensions

Directions are for sizes small (medium, large).

Back: length 10 (14, 20)" (25 [36, 51] cm), width 9 (12, 14)" (23 [30, 36] cm)

Chest: width 5 (6, 8)" (13 [15, 20] cm)

Circumference: 14 (18, 22)" (36 [46, 56] cm)

Gauge: 3 sts and 4 rows = 1" (3 cm) in stockinette stitch

4" × 4" (10 × 10 cm) swatch = 12 sts and 16 rows

Finishing

Fit points of chest piece to top edges of back piece and stitch both sides of the chest plate to the adjoining sides of the back of the sweater. Sew the ribbed portion of the chest plate to the corresponding sides of the sweater, leaving two openings at the straight sides of the chest plate to form the leg holes (sleeve openings).

Using a size K crochet hook and CC yarn, crochet two rows of single crochet from the contrast trim at the back of the neck, down the first side of the v-neck, up the other side of the v-neck, and connect to the contrast neck trim at the other side of the back of the neck. Weave in any loose ends with yarn needle.

embellished variation

varsity letter and logo sweater

A sporty variation on the V-Neck Sweater (see page 36), this timeless collegiate favorite can be knit up in your own school colors. (I have chosen Cornell University's red and white—Go Big Red!) Sew a contrasting embroidered letter, or team logo, at the center of the sweater back. Shop for these appliqués at craft and sewing stores. If you wish, embroider your own letter or logo using contrasting yarns. Add an initial or logo appliqué, and you and your canine teammate are ready for the homecoming game!

cardigan sweater

This silhouette offers long sleeves and a shorter body length that will reach full length on smaller dogs and will sit at the waist of larger dogs. This design is slightly more complicated than others in the book, as it has more pieces that you will need to sew together. Your pet will look dapper all buttoned up, and the effect is well worth your extra effort!

INSTRUCTIONS FOR
CARDIGAN SWEATER

BACK

▶ Using two strands of CC (pull one strand from inside of skein; pull second strand from outside of skein) and two strands of MC held together, cast on 26 sts. Work in garter stitch (knit every row) for two rows. Cut off the two strands of CC yarn, leaving tails of about 3" (8 cm) to be woven into the reverse side of the work using a yarn needle.

▶ Continue on right side of work using the remaining two strands of MC and work in St st, starting with a purl row, for 5" (13 cm), ending with a purl row.

▶ Continue in St st, decreasing 1 st (k2tog) at beg and end of next and all following knit rows until 12 sts remain on needle. Cut off the two threads, leaving tails, and place remaining sts on a holder.

FRONTS (make 2)

▶ Using two strands of CC and two strands of MC held together, cast on 14 sts. Work in garter stitch (knit every row) for two rows. Cut off the two strands of CC yarn, leaving tails of about 3" (8 cm) to be woven into the reverse side of the work using a yarn needle.

▶ Continue on right side of work using the remaining two strands of MC and work in St st, starting with a purl row, for 5" (13 cm) ending with a purl row.

▶ Continue in St st, decreasing 1 st (k2tog) at beg and end of next and all following knit rows until 7 sts remain on needle. Cut off the two threads, leaving tails, and place remaining sts on a holder.

▶ Work the other front piece, reversing shapings, and place the remaining 7 sts on a holder.

SLEEVES (make 2)

▶ Using two strands of CC and two strands of MC held together, cast on 14 sts. Work in garter stitch (knit every row) for two rows. Cut off the two strands of CC yarn, leaving tails of about 3" (8 cm) to be woven into the reverse side of the work using a yarn needle.

▶ Continue on right side of work using the remaining two strands of MC and work in St st, starting with a purl row, for 3" (8 cm), ending with a purl row.

▶ Continue in St st, decreasing 1 st (k2tog) at beg and end of next and all following knit rows until 2 sts remain on needle. K2tog and bind off remaining stitch.

Finishing

Make two front plackets.

Using two strands of MC and two strands of CC held together, cast on 16 sts. Knit two rows of garter stitch and bind off. Sew pieces together using yarn needle. You need to sew raglan sleeves to fronts and back; sew side seams; and sew plackets to edges of cardigan fronts and then stitch them together at the middle. Using the circular or double-pointed needles, pick up 24 sts at the collar edge of the work, between the two placket fronts. Using two strands of MC and two strands of CC held together, knit two rows of garter stitch and bind off.

Optionally, you can sew three ½" (1 cm) diameter gold buttons to the center placket: one at the top of the placket, one at the bottom of the placket, and one at the center of the placket. (This was not done in the sample shown.) Weave in any loose ends with yarn needle

MATERIALS

1 skein main color (MC) and 1 skein contrast color (CC) double knitting (DK) or sports-weight yarn, Kraemer Yarns Tatamy Tweed (45% cotton, 55% acrylic; 3.5 oz [100 g]/250 yd [229 m]) in loganberry (MC) and purple (CC) or desired colors. Two strands of yarn held together to make a bulky weight yarn

US size 11 (8 mm) straight needles; size 11 (8 mm) circular needle (16" [41 cm] length) or set of size 11 (8 mm) double-pointed needles or size to obtain gauge

Three 3 stitch holders

Optionally, three gold ½" (1 cm) diameter buttons may be sewn to the front placket

Yarn needle

Finished Dimensions

One size to fit small dogs.

Back: length 9" (23 cm), width 9" (23 cm)

Circumference: 18" (46 cm)

Gauge: 3 sts and 4 rows = 1" (3 cm) in stockinette stitch

4" × 4" (10 × 10 cm) swatch = 12 sts and 16 rows

felted tote bag

Remember the time you accidentally washed a cherished sweater in hot water? Well, what was then a cause of anguish is now a sought-after effect! Felting is the latest knitting craze. It is the simple term for the melding of fibers into a dense, solid fabric caused by heat, moisture, and agitation. First, you knit up a bag, hat, slippers, or even a decorative dog collar (see page 90) in a natural-fiber yarn suitable for felting. Do not use synthetic fibers, or washable wools, as these will not work. You will knit the garment larger than the finished article so that the natural shrinking and felting process will produce a finished item with a unique appearance. Felted knits are sturdy, which makes them the ideal choice for tote bags, such as the one shown. Embellish this bag to match any sweater shown in the book; add buttons, pom-poms, or crystals to your heart's delight. Carry a knitting project, a small dog, or your pet's toys, treats, and bowls for a trip away from home. Rest assured that felting makes a strong fabric and your precious cargo will be secure!

INSTRUCTIONS FOR
FELTED
TOTE BAG

BOTTOM OF BAG

Using three strands held together, cast on 30 sts onto straight needle. Work in garter stitch (knit every row) for 20 rows. Leave on needle.

SIDES OF BAG

▶ Using circular needle, pick up 10 sts on short side of work, then pick up 30 sts on cast-on, long side of work, and then pick up 10 sts on other short side of work.

▶ Using circular needle, knit the 30 sts still left on straight needle and continue around the base until all stitches are on the circular needle and the first circular row is complete. Place a marker here to indicate the start of the row.

▶ Cut off one of the strands of yarn, leaving a tail to be woven into the work, and continue knitting circular rows to form the body of the bag using two strands of the yarn held together. (Three strands were used for the base so that it will be thicker and sturdier when the work is complete.) Knit until sides measure 18" (46 cm) in height and then bind off. Weave in any loose ends with yarn needle.

HANDLES (knit 2)

▶ Take two double-pointed needles from the set and, using two strands of yarn, cast 7 stitches onto one of them. Do not turn work, but slide stitches back to the other side of the needle.

▶ *Taking the yarn firmly across the back of work, k7. Slide stitches back to other side of needle.* Repeat from * to * until strap measures 30" (76 cm) and bind off. Knit another identical strap.

Finishing

Using the same yarn as was used to knit the bag, sew the handles to the top edge of the tote bag, centering the handles on the longer sides of the bag, and leaving about 6" (15 cm) between two ends of each handle. Be sure that the handles are not twisted before attaching them to the body of the bag. Sew about 2" (5 cm) of ends of straps inside the bag so that it will be secure when felted.

Felting Technique

Place the assembled tote bag, right side out, into a net lingerie bag. Follow the general felting instructions on page 19.

Because the base of the bag was knit with three strands of yarn, proportionate to the sides and handles of the bag, it may require more finely tuned shaping during the felting process. I found it useful to hold the base under a stream of hot water from the sink, for several counts, to aid in the shrinking process. Scrunching the base tighter (by hand) was also effective in achieving the correct sizing.

Rinse the bag in clear water and let dry completely before sewing on the trim. If the bag dries to the wrong size, you may place it back into a hot wash to adjust the size slightly.

Trim

This bag can be knit to match any sweater that is made with Mauch Chunky in this book. We are showing a black pearls design. For this design, stitch an assortment of pearls onto the finished tote bag in an appealing manner.

MATERIALS

- 8 skeins bulky weight yarn, Kraemer Yarns Mauch Chunky (100% wool; 3.5 oz [100 g]/120 yd [110 m]) in black or desired color

- US size 15 (10 mm) straight needles; size 15 (10 mm) circular needle (30" [76 cm] length); 1 set of size 13 (9 mm) double-pointed needles or size to obtain gauge

- Stitch marker

- Yarn needle

Finished Dimensions

Bag: As originally knit: length 18" (46 cm), width 10" (25 cm), height 18" (46 cm)

After washing and felting: length 13" (33 cm), width 6" (15 cm), height 9" (23 cm)

Straps (make 2): Length as originally knit: 30" [76 cm]

Length as felted: 18" (46 cm)

Chapter Two

preppy puppy

preppy puppy

The following four patterns were inspired by the clothes of a famous dogwear designer, **"Ruff Lauren,"** who is known for classic American styles that epitomize good taste and good breeding. Use these patterns to coordinate your look with your pet's. You can knit these designs in the yarns shown here for a sporty effect, or choose a precious fiber—such as cashmere, alpaca, or merino wool—for a luxurious treat. You (and your pooch) deserve the best!

cable rib sweater

This classic look is fetching on both male and female dogs. Likewise, the matching muffler is popular with both women and men. Have fun with the selection of color. The cable pattern looks best in solid-colored yarns, especially those with no additional texture.

INSTRUCTIONS FOR
CABLE RIB SWEATER

BACK

Starting at hem edge, cast on 32 (38, 44) sts and work garter stitch (knit every row) for four rows. Follow the instructions below for the cable pattern:

Row 1 (RS): K1, p1, *k4, p2; repeat from * to last 2 sts, p1, k1.

Row 2 (WS): P1, k1, *p4, k2; repeat from * to last s sts, k1, p1.

Row 3 (RS; this is the cable row): K1, p1, *place next 2 sts onto cable needle and hold in front, k next 2 sts, k 2 from cable needle, p2; repeat from * to last 2 sts, p1, k1.

Row 4 (WS): Repeat Row 2.

Repeat Rows 1 through 4 until piece measures 8 (12, 18)" (20 [30, 46] cm) from beginning, ending with Row 3 of pattern.

Next Row: Purl, increasing (2, 0, 2) sts evenly spaced.

To form turtleneck, follow these two rows for 4" (10 cm):

Row 1 (RS): *K2, p2; repeat from * to last 2 sts, k2.

Row 2 (WS): *P2, k2; repeat from * to last 2 sts, p2.

Bind off in rib pattern, leaving a length of yarn to be used to sew together the sweater.

CHEST

Cast on 16 (20, 24) sts. Work in 2 x 2 rib (k2, p2) every row for 2" (5 cm).

Change to St st and work for 2 (3, 4)" (5 [8, 10] cm). Continue in St st, decreasing 1 st (k2tog) at the beg and end of each following knit row until 2 sts remains on needle. Cut yarn and pull end through last 2 sts to fasten off, leaving a length attached to chest plate to be used to sew together the chest of sweater.

Finishing

For back piece, use length of yarn to sew together turtleneck of sweater. Leave yarn connected at bottom edge of turtleneck. Fit point of chest piece under seam at bottom of turtleneck and stitch both sides of the triangle to the adjoining sides of the back of the sweater. Sew the ribbed portion of the chest plate to the corresponding sides of the sweater, leaving two openings at the straight sides of the chest plate to form the leg holes (sleeve openings). Weave in any loose ends with yarn needle.

MATERIALS

1 skein bulky weight yarn, Kraemer Yarns Mauch Chunky (100% wool; 3.5 oz [100 g]/120 yd [110 m]) in kiwi or desired color

US size 11 (8 mm) straight needles or size to obtain gauge

Cable needle

Yarn needle

Finished Dimensions

Directions are for sizes small (medium, large).

Back: length 10 (14, 20)" (25 [36, 51] cm), 4" (10 cm) turtleneck, width 10 (12, 14)" (25 [30, 36] cm)

Chest: width 5 (6.5, 8)" (13 [17, 20] cm)

Circumference: 15 (18.5, 22)" (38 [47, 56] cm)

Gauge: 3 sts and 4 rows = 1" (3 cm) in stockinette stitch

unisex cable rib muffler

This design is a favorite of both men and women. Men may prefer a shorter length muffler, while women might prefer a length that can be wrapped around the neck several times. Another way to wear this muffler is by folding it in half. Pull the folded end to the side front of your neck, and pull the two loose ends through the loop formed by the folded end. This creates a jaunty, casual look for both men and women.

INSTRUCTIONS FOR
CABLE RIB MUFFLER

Starting at hem edge, cast on 20 sts. Work in garter stitch (knit every row) for four rows. Follow the instructions below for the cable pattern:

*Row 1 (RS): K6, p2, k4, p2, k6.

Row 2 (WS): P6, k2, p4, k2, p6.

Repeat rows 1 and 2 three more times (eight rows in pattern, total).

Row 3 (RS; this is the cable row): K2, *place next 2 sts onto cable needle held in front of work, knit next 2 sts, k2 sts off cable needle, p2 and repeat from * to end of row.

Row 4 (WS): P6, k2, p4, k2, p6.*

Repeat pattern between * until you have reached the desired length of your scarf. Knit four rows in garter stitch and bind off. Weave in any loose ends with yarn needle.

MATERIALS

- 2 skeins bulky weight yarn, Kraemer Yarns Mauch Chunky (100% wool; 3.5 oz [100 g]/120 yd [110 m]) in kiwi or desired color
- US size 11 (8 mm) straight needles or size to obtain gauge
- Cable needle
- Yarn needle

Finished Dimensions

5" wide × 48" long (13 × 122 cm), but you can knit this to any length you choose.

Gauge: 3 sts = 1" (3 cm) in stockinette stitch

center cable sweater

This design features a bold cable at the center of the dog's back. It is matched in the muffler design (see page 54). This design looks good on both male and female dogs. The corresponding muffler looks equally good on both men and women.

INSTRUCTIONS FOR
CENTER CABLE SWEATER

BACK

Starting at hem edge, cast on 26 (34, 42) sts. Work in garter stitch (knit every row) for eight rows. Follow instructions below for cable pattern:

Row 1 (RS): K6 (10, 14), p3, k8, p3, k6 (10, 14).

Row 2 (WS): P6 (10, 14), k3, p8, k3, p6 (10, 14).

Repeat rows 1 and 2 three more times (eight rows in pattern, total).

Row 3 (RS; this is the cable row): K6 (10, 14), p3, place next 4 sts onto cable needle held in front of work, knit next 4 sts, k4 sts off cable needle, p3, k6 (10, 14).

Row 4 (WS): P6, (10, 14), k3, p8, k3, p6 (10, 14).

Repeat rows 1 and 2 four times (eight rows in pattern, total).

Repeat rows 3 and 4 once.

Continue in this pattern, cabling every eighth row, until piece measures 8 (12, 18)" (20 [30, 46] cm) from the end of the hem edge (not including these garter stitch rows in your measurement) to form body of sweater.

To form turtleneck, follow these two rows for 4" (10 cm):

Row 1 (RS): *K2, p2, rep from * across row, k2.

Row 2 (WS): *P2, k2, rep from * across row, p2.

Bind off in this rib stitch pattern, leaving a length of yarn to be used to sew together the sweater.

CHEST

Cast on 16 (18, 24) sts. For sizes small and large, work in 2 × 2 rib (k2, p2 every row) for 2" (5 cm). For size medium, work as follows for 2" (5 cm):

Row 1 (RS): *K2, p2, rep from * across row, k2.

Row 2 (WS): *P2, k2, rep from * across row, p2.

Change to St st and work for 1 (2, 3)" (3 [5, 8] cm). Continue in St st, decreasing 1 st (k2tog) at beg and end of each following knit row until 1 st remains on needle. Cut and pull end of yarn through the stitch to fasten off work at point of triangle, leaving a length attached to chest plate to be used to sew together the chest of sweater.

Finishing

For back piece, use length of yarn to sew together turtleneck of sweater. Leave yarn connected at bottom edge of turtleneck. Fit point of chest piece under seam at bottom of turtleneck and stitch both sides of the triangle to the adjoining sides of the back of the sweater. Sew the ribbed portion of the chest plate to the corresponding sides of the sweater, leaving two openings at the straight sides of the chest plate to form the leg holes (sleeve openings). Weave in any loose ends with yarn needle.

MATERIALS

1 skein bulky weight yarn, Kraemer Yarns Mauch Chunky (100% wool; 3.5 oz [100 g]/120 yd [110 m]) in raspberry or desired color

US size 11 (8 mm) straight needles or size to obtain gauge

Cable needle

Yarn needle

Finished Dimensions

Directions are for sizes small (medium, large).

Back: length 10 (14, 20)" (25 [36, 51] cm), 4" (10 cm) turtleneck, width 9 (12, 14)" (23 [30, 36] cm)

Chest: width 5 (6, 8)" (13 [15, 20] cm)

Circumference: 14 (18, 22)" (36 [46, 56] cm)

Gauge: 3 sts and 4 rows = 1" (3 cm) in stockinette stitch

unisex center cable muffler

This cable design also looks beautiful when knit in luxury yarns, such as merino wool, alpaca, or cashmere. The cable design is most evident when knit with a solid-colored yarn without textural interest. But, rules are meant to be broken, so feel free to knit this design in a tweed yarn with lots of texture and flecks of color, if this pleases your sense of style.

INSTRUCTIONS FOR
UNISEX CENTER CABLE MUFFLER

Starting at hem edge, cast on 20 sts. Work in garter stitch (knit every row) for eight rows. Follow instructions below for cable pattern:

*Row 1 (RS): K4, p2, k8, p2, k4.

Row 2 (WS): K6, p8, k6.

Repeat rows 1 and 2 three more times (eight rows in pattern, total).

Row 3 (RS; this is the cable row): K4, p2, place next 4 sts onto cable needle held in front of work, k next 4 sts, k4 sts off cable needle, p2, k4.

Row 4 (WS): K6, p8, k6.*

Repeat pattern between * until you have reached the desired length of your scarf. Knit eight rows in garter stitch and bind off. Weave in any loose ends with yarn needle.

MATERIALS

- 2 skeins bulky weight yarn, Kraemer Yarns Mauch Chunky (100% wool; 3.5 oz [100 g]/120 yd [110 m]) in raspberry or desired color
- US size 11 (8 mm) straight needles or size to obtain gauge
- Cable needle
- Yarn needle

Finished Dimensions

5" wide × 72" long (13 × 183 cm), but you can knit this to any length you choose.

Gauge: 3 sts = 1" (3 cm) in stockinette stitch

eyelet and ribbon sweater

Knit this dressy sweater in your favorite colors, or choose classic cream and black. Embellish this piece with a selection of beautiful ribbons. Choose from satins or grosgrains, patterns or solids, and try metallic ones, as shown here, for a formal look. Collect lots of ribbons, and change your pet's outfit by simply lacing a new ribbon through the eyelet holes!

INSTRUCTIONS FOR
EYELET HOLE AND RIBBON SWEATER

BACK

Cast on 26 (34, 42) sts. Work in seed stitch as follows for 1" (3 cm), ending with a WS row:

Row 1: K1, p1, repeat across row.

Row 2: P1, k1, repeat across row.

Change to St st and work for 5 (7, 10)" (13 [18, 25] cm).

Next row RS: *K2, k2tog* and repeat from * to * across row.

Next row WS: P2, *make 1, P3* and repeat from * to * across row, ending in purl stitches.

Change to St st and work even until piece measures 10 (14, 20)" (25 [36, 51] cm) to form body of sweater (not counting the seed stitch edging in your measurement), ending in a purl row. Work in seed stitch for 1" (3 cm) and bind off, leaving a length of yarn to be used to sew together the sweater.

CHEST

Cast on 16 (18, 24) sts. Work in seed stitch as follows for 1" (3 cm), ending with a WS row:

Row 1: K1, p1, repeat across row.

Row 2: P1, k1, repeat across row.

Change to St st and work for 2 (3, 5)" (5 [8, 13] cm). Continue in St st decreasing 1 st (k2tog) at beg and end of each following knit row until 1 st remains on needle. Cut and pull end of yarn through the stitch to fasten off work at point of triangle, leaving a length of yarn attached to chest plate to be used to sew together the chest of sweater.

Finishing

For back piece, use length of yarn to sew together crewneck of sweater. Leave yarn connected at bottom edge of crewneck. Fit point of chest piece under seam at bottom of neck and stitch both sides of the triangle to the adjoining sides of the back of the sweater. Sew the ribbed portion of the chest plate to the corresponding sides of the sweater, leaving two openings at the straight sides of the chest plate to form the leg holes (sleeve openings). Weave in any loose ends with yarn needle.

Starting in the middle of back, thread a 36" (91 cm) length of ³/₄" (2 cm) -wide ribbon through the eyelet holes on one side of the back of the sweater, loop it under the wrong side of the

sweater back, and continue to lace it through the holes at the other side of the sweater back; tie it in a bow at center back.

MATERIALS

- 1 skein worsted-weight yarn, Kraemer Yarns (100% merino super-wash wool; 3.5 oz [100 g]/230 yd [210 m]) in pearl or desired color
- US size 11 (8 mm) straight needles or size to obtain gauge
- Yarn needle

Finished Dimensions

Directions are for sizes small (medium, large).

Back: length 10 (14, 20)" (25 [36, 51] cm), 1" (3 cm) crewneck, width 9 (12, 14)" (23 [30, 36] cm)

Chest: width 5 (6, 8)" (13 [15, 20] cm)

Circumference: 14 (18, 22)" (36 [46, 56] cm)

Gauge: 3 sts and 4 rows = 1" (3 cm) in stockinette stitch

4" × 4" (10 × 10 cm) swatch = 12 sts and 16 rows

hoodie sweater

What do you wear in the "hood?" Choose this pattern for your urban pooch. A classic hooded sweatshirt shapes up quickly in bulky yarn. Use a neutral color, as shown here, for basic sweats, or softer colors for higher fashion. Luxury yarns will work well too; try cashmere or merino wool for a jolt of cutting-edge style.

INSTRUCTIONS FOR
HOODIE SWEATER

BACK

Cast on 26 (34, 42) sts. Work as follows for 1" (3 cm):

Row 1 (RS): *K2, p2, rep from * across row, k2.

Row 2 (WS): *P2, k2, rep from * across row, p2.

Change to St st and work until piece measures 10 (14, 20)" (25 [36, 51] cm) to form body of sweater, ending in a purl row. Place marker or mark with a safety pin. Continue to knit in St st for another 5 (7, 10)" (13 [18, 25] cm) to form hood of sweater. Bind off, leaving a length of yarn to be used to sew together the sweater.

CHEST

Cast on 16 (18, 24) sts. For sizes small and large, work in 2 × 2 rib (k2, p2 every row) for 1" (3 cm). For size medium, work as follows for 1" (3 cm):

Row 1 (RS): *K2, p2, rep from * across row, k2.

Row 2 (WS): *P2, k2, rep from * across row, p2.

Change to St st and work for 2 (3, 5)" (5 [8, 13] cm). Continue in St st, decreasing 1 st (k2tog) at beg and end of each following knit row until 1 st remains on needle. Cut and pull end of yarn through the stitch to fasten off work at point of triangle, leaving a length of yarn attached to chest plate to be used to sew together the chest of sweater.

Finishing

For back piece, use length of yarn to sew together top of hood of sweater. Fit point of chest piece at bottom of neck (where marker or safety pin was placed) and stitch both sides of the triangle to the adjoining sides of the back of the sweater. Sew the ribbed portion of the chest plate to the corresponding sides of the sweater, leaving two openings at the straight sides of the chest plate to form the leg holes (sleeve openings).

Taking the crochet hook and yarn, crochet a chain 20 (22, 24)" (51 [56, 61] cm). Beginning at bottom of hood (where marker or safety pin was placed) and 2 sts in from the edge, thread chain in on one side of bottom of hood front and out at the same spot on the other side. Leave hood with pull strings loose or tie in a bow. Weave in any loose ends with yarn needle.

MATERIALS

1 skein bulky weight yarn, Kraemer Yarns Mauch Chunky (100% wool; 3.5 oz [100 g]/120 yd [110 m]) shitake or desired color

US size 11 (8 mm) straight needles or size to obtain gauge

Crochet hook size K

Stitch marker or safety pin

Yarn needle

Finished Dimensions

Directions are for sizes small (medium, large).

Back: length 10 (14, 20)" (25 [36, 51] cm), 5 (7, 10)" (13 [18, 25] cm) hood, width 9 (12, 14)" (23 [30, 36] cm)

Chest: width 5 (6, 8)" (13 [15, 20] cm)

Circumference: 14 (18, 22)" (36 [46, 56] cm)

Gauge: 3 sts and 4 rows = 1" (3 cm) in stockinette stitch

4" × 4" (10 × 10 cm) swatch = 12 sts and 16 rows

Chapter Three

pet patterns

pet patterns

Does your dog go dotty for diamonds?

Gaga for grids?

Yikes, stripes!

Go graphic!

The following six projects will be perfect for your pet!

diamond turtleneck sweater

Try this clean, graphic design on your pet. Solid-colored dogs look smashing in this color combination. The pattern also works well if in colors compatible with your animal's coat.

INSTRUCTIONS FOR
DIAMOND TURTLENECK SWEATER

BACK

▶ Using MC, starting at hem edge, cast on 36 (48, 56) sts. Work in 2 × 2 rib (k2, p2 every row) for 2 (2, 3)" (5 [5, 8] cm) to form ribbing at hem.

▶ Work in St st for 8 (12, 17)" (20 [30, 43] cm) for body of sweater, following chart as directed below.

▶ Create one bobbin of CC for each diamond appearing in the sweater. When switching from MC to CC, twist yarns to minimize any gaps between colors. (See page 74, Working with Color, for more on creating bobbins.) For size small, work in St st in MC for six rows, then begin chart. Knit 1 st in MC, then begin to follow chart for five repeats (1 repeat = 7 stitches). Reverse spacing on WS rows, starting chart at beginning of row and following chart with 1 st in MC. Repeat chart for three lengthwise repeats

(1 repeat = 15 rows), then work in St st for six rows in MC until piece measures 10" (25 cm). Then begin to work turtleneck.

▶ For size medium, work in St st in MC for four rows, then begin chart. K3 sts in MC, then begin to follow chart for six repeats, then k3 sts in MC. Reverse spacing on WS rows. Repeat chart for four lengthwise repeats, then St st for four rows until piece measures 14" (36 cm). Then begin to work turtleneck.

▶ For size large, St st in MC for four rows, then begin chart. Knit eight repeats of chart. Repeat chart for seven lengthwise repeats, then St st for four rows until piece measures 20" (51 cm). Then begin to work turtleneck.

▶ For turtleneck, work in 2 × 2 rib for 4" (10 cm). Bind off in rib stitch, leaving a length of yarn attached to be used to sew together the sweater.

CHEST

▶ In MC, starting at hem edge, cast on 20 (24, 32) sts. Work in 2 × 2 rib for 2 (2, 3)" (5 [5, 8] cm) to form ribbing at hem.

▶ Change to St st and work for 1 (2, 3)" (3 [5, 8] cm). Continue in St st and decrease 1 st (k2tog) at beg and end of all following knit rows until 1 st remains on needle. Cut and pull yarn through remaining loop to fasten at point of triangle.

MATERIALS

1 skein main color (MC) and 1 skein contrast color (CC) worsted-weight yarn, Kraemer Yarns Summit Hill (100% merino superwash wool; 3.5 oz [100 g]/230 yd [210 m]) in pearl (MC) and obsidian (CC) or desired colors

US size 9 (5.5 mm) straight needles or size to obtain gauge

Yarn needle

Crochet hook (optional)

Pattern graph (page 119)

Finished Dimensions

Directions are for sizes small (medium, large).

Back: length 10 (14, 20)" (25 [36, 51] cm), 4" (10 cm) turtleneck, width 9 (12, 14)" (23 [30, 36] cm)

Chest: width 5 (6, 8)" (13 [15, 20] cm)

Circumference: 14 (18, 22)" (36 [46, 56] cm)

Gauge: 4 sts and 6 rows = 1" (3 cm) in stockinette stitch

4" × 4" (10 × 10 cm) swatch = 16 sts and 24 rows

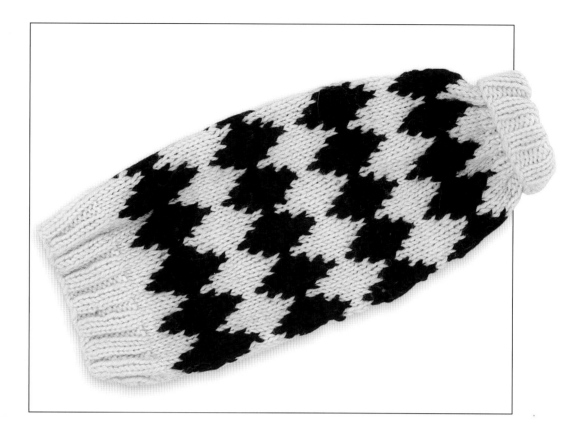

Finishing

Starting at the turtleneck end of the back, use the attached length of yarn to sew together the ribbed portion to form the neck of the sweater. Do not cut the loose end of yarn when you are done. It will be used to sew the chest to the back of the sweater. Fit the triangular portion of the chest piece under this turtleneck and use the remaining yarn to sew one side of the triangular form to the adjoining stockinette stitch portion of the back piece. Fasten yarn here securely and conceal end by pulling needle through a few stitches at the reverse side of the garment. Cut yarn.

Use the length of yarn at the top of the triangle to sew the other triangular portion of the chest to the back. Conceal end of yarn as described above and cut off. Thread a length of matching yarn through your needle and sew the ribbed portion of the chest piece to the adjoining sides of the back piece, making the chest piece lie flat against the back portion of the sweater. This will leave two openings, one at each side, to accommodate the dog's legs (armholes). Weave in any loose ends with yarn needle.

If you wish, you may use a crochet hook to attach a new length of yarn ½" (1 cm) from the center of the hem. Chain a length about 1" (3 cm) long and attach other end at the point ½" (1 cm) from the center on the other side. This will create a loop through which you can pull the dog's tail to secure the sweater to your pet at the hem of the garment.

grid turtleneck sweater

Think—and dress—out of the box! In this pattern, a graph paper grid is worked across the back of a turtleneck sweater to add geometric detail to the basic design. It's the perfect way to underscore your dog's fashion sense.

MATERIALS

- 1 skein main color (MC) and 1 skein contrast color (CC) worsted-weight yarn, Kraemer Yarns Summit Hill (100% merino superwash wool; 3.5 oz [100 g]/230 yd [210 m]) in pearl (MC) and ruby (CC) or desired colors
- US size 9 (5.5 mm) straight needles or size to obtain gauge
- Yarn needle
- Crochet hook (optional)

Finished Dimensions

Directions are for sizes small (medium, large).

- **Back:** length 10 (14, 20)" (25 [36, 51] cm), 4" (10 cm) turtleneck, width 9 (12, 14)" (23 [30, 36] cm)
- **Chest:** width 5 (6, 8)" (13 [15, 20] cm)
- **Circumference:** 14 (18, 22)" (36 [46, 56] cm)

- **Gauge:** 4 sts and 6 rows = 1" (3 cm) in stockinette stitch
- 4" × 4" (10 × 10 cm) swatch = 16 sts and 24 rows

INSTRUCTIONS FOR
GRID TURTLENECK SWEATER

BACK

▶ Starting with MC at hem edge, cast on 36 (48, 56) sts. Work in 2 × 2 rib (k2, p2 every row) for 2 (2, 3)" (5 [5, 8] cm) to form ribbing at hem.

▶ Start pattern: Change to CC and knit one row in St st. Change to MC and knit next five rows in St st. Follow this pattern for the next 42 (66, 96) rows, until piece measures 10 (14, 20)" (25 [36, 51] cm).

▶ Using MC, work in 2 × 2 rib for 4" (10 cm) to create turtleneck of sweater. Bind off in rib stitch, leaving a length of yarn attached to be used to sew together the sweater.

▶ Using a length of CC yarn thread through a needle, use duplicate stitch to create the lengthwise stripes of the grid, starting at the 1st (1st, 2nd) stitch in the row and skipping 5 sts between each contrast stripe, ending at the last (last, next to last) stitch at the end of the row.

CHEST

▶ Starting with MC at hem edge, cast on 20 (24, 32) sts. Work in 2 × 2 rib (k2, p2 every row) for 2 (2, 3)" (5 [5, 8] cm) to form ribbing at hem.

▶ Change to St st and work for 4 (4, 5)" (10 [10, 13] cm). Continue

in St st, decreasing 1 st (k2tog) at beg and end of all following knit rows until 1 st remains on the needle. Cut and pull yarn through remaining loop to fasten at point of triangle.

Finishing

Starting at the turtleneck end of the back, use the attached length of yarn to sew together the ribbed portion to form the neck of the sweater. Do not cut the loose end of yarn when you are done. It will be used to sew the chest to the back of the sweater. Fit the triangular portion of the chest piece under this turtleneck and use the remaining yarn to sew one side of the triangular form to the adjoining stockinette stitch portion of the back piece. Fasten yarn here securely and conceal end by pulling needle through a few stitches at the reverse side of the garment. Cut yarn.

Use the length of yarn at the top of the triangle to sew the other triangular portion of the chest to the back. Conceal end of yarn as described above and cut off. Thread a length of matching yarn through your needle and sew the ribbed portion of the chest piece to the adjoining sides of the back piece, making the chest piece lie flat against the back portion of the sweater. This will leave two openings, one at each side, to accommodate the dog's legs (armholes). Weave in any loose ends with yarn needle.

If you wish, you may use a crochet hook to attach a new length of yarn ½" (1 cm) from the center of the hem. Chain a length about 1" (3 cm) long and attach other end at the point ½" (1 cm) from the center on the other side. This will create a loop through which you can pull the dog's tail to secure the sweater to your pet at the hem of the garment.

striped bulky turtleneck sweater

This sporty look is perfect for leisure activities. You can knit this sweater in bright colors, muted tones, or a combination of both, as shown here.

INSTRUCTIONS FOR
STRIPED BULKY TURTLENECK SWEATER

BACK

Using one of the colors (color 1), cast on 26 (34, 42) sts. Work in 2 × 2 rib as follows for 2" (5 cm):

Row 1 (RS): *K2, p2, rep from * across row, k2.

Row 2 (WS): *P2, k2, rep from * across row, p2.

Change to other color (color 2) and work in St st for 2" (5 cm). Change back to color 1 and work in St st for 2" (5 cm). Continue to work in St st, alternating stripe colors every 2" (5 cm) until piece measures 10 (14, 20)" (25 [36, 51] cm), ending in a purl row. Using next color in sequence, work in 2 × 2 rib for 4" (10 cm) to form turtleneck of sweater. Bind off in rib, leaving a length of yarn to be used to sew together the sweater.

CHEST

Using opposite color from ribbed hemline at back of sweater (color 2), cast on 16 (18, 24) sts. For sizes small and large, work in 2 × 2 rib (k2, p2 every row) for 2" (5 cm). For size medium, work as follows for 2" (5 cm):

Row 1 (RS): *K2, p2, rep from * across row, k2.

Row 2 (WS): *P2, k2, rep from * across row, p2.

Change to St st and work for 1 (2, 4)" (3 [5, 10] cm), being sure to change color every 2" (5 cm) in sequence. Continuing to follow color sequence, work in St st, decreasing 1 st (k2tog) at beg and end of all following knit rows until 1 st remains on needle. Cut and pull end of yarn

through the stitch to fasten off work at point of triangle. Cut off remaining yarn, leaving a length attached to chest plate to be used to sew together the chest of sweater.

Finishing

For back piece, use length of yarn to sew together turtleneck of sweater. Leave yarn connected at bottom edge of turtleneck. Fit point of chest piece under seam at bottom of

neck, matching up stripes, and stitch both sides of the triangle to the adjoining sides of the back of the sweater. Sew the ribbed portion of the chest plate to the corresponding sides of the sweater, leaving two openings at the straight sides of the chest plate to form the leg holes (sleeve openings). Weave in any loose ends with yarn needle.

MATERIALS

1 skein bulky weight yarn, Kraemer Yarns Mauch Chunky (100% wool; 3.5 oz [100 g]/120 yd [110 m]) in two desired colors; blue raspberry and portobello used here

US size 11 (8 mm) straight needles or size to obtain gauge

Yarn needle

Finished Dimensions

Directions are for sizes small (medium, large).

Back: length 10 (14, 20)" (25 [36, 51] cm), 4" (10 cm) turtleneck, width 9 (12, 14)" (23 [30, 36] cm)

Chest: width 5 (6, 8)" (13 [15, 20] cm)

Circumference: 14 (18, 22)" (36 [46, 56] cm)

Gauge: 3 sts and 4 rows = 1" (3 cm) in stockinette stitch

4" × 4" (10 × 10 cm) swatch = 12 sts and 16 rows

fair isle sweater

The Fair Isle is a classic British design popularized by the Duke of Windsor. It is both sporty and elegant. This particular pattern was inspired by a vintage dog sweater I bought while traveling abroad. The bright colors shown are a vibrant choice, but you can select muted tones, if you prefer. This is a more complicated pattern than some of the others in the book, and it is suitable for more experienced knitters. Try it if you are ready to expand your abilities.

INSTRUCTIONS FOR
FAIR ISLE SWEATER

BACK

▶ Using color 1 (butter-nut) and starting at hem edge, cast on 26 (34, 42) sts.

▶ As the repeat of the chart is 4 sts wide, the following instructions apply. All sizes will begin and end with 1 edge st—this st should be knit in the same color as the st next to it. The edge stitches will be sewn into the seams. For size small begin with 1 edge st, work six repeats of chart, and end with 1 edge st. For size medium begin with

1 edge st, work eight repeats of chart, and end with 1 edge st. For size large begin with 1 edge st, work ten repeats of chart, and end with 1 edge st.

▶ For sizes small and large begin to follow chart at Row 1. For size small, follow chart one time until piece measures 10" (25 cm); for size large follow chart two times until piece measures 20" (51 cm). For size

medium work six rows in color 1, follow chart one time, then work more rows of color 1 until piece measures 14" (36 cm).

▶ Following chart, work as follows for 6 rows:

Row 1 (RS): *K2, p2, rep from * across row, k2.

Row 2 (WS): *P2, k2, rep from * across row, p2.

▶ Change to St st and complete color chart as described above for your size.

▶ Using color 1, work as follows for 1" (3 cm) to form crewneck of sweater:

Row 1 (RS): *K2, p2, rep from * across row, k2.

Row 2 (WS): *P2, k2, rep from * across row, p2.

Bind off in rib pattern, leaving a length of yarn to be used to sew together the sweater.

CHEST

▶ Using color 1, cast on 18 (22, 26) sts. All sizes will begin and end with 1 edge st— this st should be knit in the same color as the st next to it. The edge stitches will be sewn into the seams. For size small begin with 1 edge st, work four repeats of chart, and end with 1 edge st. For size medium begin with 1 edge st, work five repeats of chart, and end with 1 edge

st. For size large begin with 1 edge st, work six repeats of chart, and end with 1 edge st.

▶ Following sleeve chart, work as follows for 6 rows:

Row 1 (RS): *K2, p2, rep from * across row, k2.

Row 2 (WS): *P2, k2, rep from * across row, p2.

▶ Change to St st and work through chart the same as for back.

▶ Using color 1, work as follows for 1" (3 cm) to form crewneck of sweater:

Row 1 (RS): *K2, p2, rep from * across row, k2.

Row 2 (WS): *P2, k2, rep from * across row, p2.

Bind off in rib pattern, leaving a length of yarn to be used to sew together the sweater.

SLEEVES (make two)

▶ Using color 1, cast on 26 (38, 50) sts. All sizes will begin and end with 1 edge st— this st should be knit in the same color as the st next to it. The edge stitches will be sewn into the seams. For size small begin with 1 edge st, work six repeats of chart, and end with 1 edge st.

For size medium begin with 1 edge st, work nine repeats of chart, and end with 1 edge st. For size large begin with 1 edge st, work twelve repeats of chart, and end with 1 edge st.

▶ Following sleeve chart, work as follows for 6 rows:

Row 1 (RS): *K2, p2, rep from * across row, k2.

Row 2 (WS): *P2, k2, rep from * across row, p2.

▶ Change to St st and continue to follow chart. For size small follow chart one time. For size medium follow chart one time and work 4 more rows in color 1. For size large follow chart one time and work 8 more rows in color 1.

Bind off, leaving a length of yarn to be used to sew the sleeves to the sweater.

Finishing

Use length of yarn to sew together the front and back of sweater at the crewneck. Sew front to back beginning at bottom rib, leaving a 4 (6, 8)" (10 [15, 20] cm) opening on each side to form the leg holes (sleeve openings). Sew sleeves to sleeve openings. Weave in loose ends with yarn needle.

MATERIALS

1 skein bulky weight yarn, Kraemer Yarns Mauch Chunky (100% wool; 3.5 oz [100 g]/120 yds [110 m]) in each of the following colors: 1. butternut (gold), 2. pumpkin (orange), 3. raspberry (bright pink), 4. white, 5. kiwi (lime green) 6. walnut (brown), 7. pine nut (dark green), or desired colors

US size 11 (8 mm) straight needles or size to obtain gauge

Yarn needle

Pattern graph (page 120)

Finished Dimensions

Directions are for sizes small (medium, large).

Back: length 10 (14, 20)" (25 [36, 51] cm), 1" (3 cm) crewneck, width 8 (11, 13)" (20 [28, 33] cm)

Chest: width 5 (6.5, 8)" (13 [17, 20] cm)

Circumference: 13 (17.5, 21)" (33 [44.5, 53] cm)

Gauge: 3 sts and 4 rows = 1" (3 cm) in stockinette stitch

4" × 4" (10 × 10 cm) swatch = 12 sts and 16 rows

Working with Color

Color can be incorporated into your knitting in many ways. Solid-colored garments, using only one strand of yarn, are the simplest and most basic use of color. A tweed effect can be easily created by holding two different colored or textured strands of yarn together and knitting them as one. Stripes are another way to introduce color to your work.

Knitting patterns of two or more colors is easy, even for beginners. The multicolored patterns featured in this book are created by two basic methods, intarsia and Fair Isle. Intarsia is the technique of introducing blocks of color (or colors) to a basic knitting fabric. The Diamond Turtleneck sweater (page 64) is an example of intarsia knitting. Fair Isle is a repeating pattern of rows of mostly horizontal elements and smaller motifs. The Fair Isle sweater (page 76) and the Peruvian sweater (page 80) are examples of this technique. Both techniques are accomplished by knitting rows from the ball of your main color and knitting the required patterned stitches from bobbins of contrasting colored yarn. (Bobbins can be purchased from yarn and craft stores or can be homemade from small pieces of cardboard. The strands of yarn you are working with can also be kept neat by tying a loose knot around each gathered length of yarn.)

In most cases, as in this book, the multicolored pattern to be followed is drawn on a chart that accompanies the written pattern instructions. The chart appears on

a graph paper grid, and each box represents a single stitch in the design. The graph boxes are shown as square, when in actuality, knit stitches are wider than they are tall, so take this into account when you are drawing your own charts for knitting, or your resulting design may appear too short and wide. The boxes may be colored in with the color of the yarn to be used, or a symbol such as a dot or dash may designate each of the colors in the final design.

To follow the chart, you must first knit the number of rows or inches in the main yarn color, as instructed in the written portion of the pattern. Some charts plot out the entire sweater. Other charts are simply a small graph of just the design motif itself, and it is up to the knitter to begin to work the chart when designated in the written instructions. To read a chart, start at the bottom row, because you work your knitting from the hem up. On knit rows (right side rows), follow the chart from right to left in the same manner that your stitches are worked from the needles. On purl rows (wrong side rows), follow the chart from left to right, as if you were reading.

One simple tip is to photocopy the charts and work from the copy. I like to cross out each completed row with a crayon, so I always know where in the chart to continue work. If you work from a copy, you will not ruin the chart in the book for the next time you might choose to knit the pattern. It is also a good idea to use a ruler or index card held directly below the row in which you are working, to avoid confusion by blocking out the previously worked rows.

When knitting a row with more than one color, it is a good idea to let go of each of the yarns after you have knit it, letting the yarn strand hang loosely at the back of your work. Take the yarn in the new color and pull it under and over the previously worked yarn before knitting with it. In this way, you are winding the two yarns around each other once, which will prevent the formation of holes in your work. Carry the unused yarn(s) behind your work until you need to knit that color again. If the resulting span of yarn, called a float, is going to be long, be sure to wrap it around the color you are knitting with, as just described, every few stitches so that it does not hang loosely from the back of the garment. Long floats are prone to snagging when the garment is put on or taken off, and even more so in the case of a dog, so this is a good tip to follow.

peruvian turtleneck sweater

On my trip to Peru several years ago, I saw many beautiful examples of this folk design and was inspired to create my own version. The electric colors are typical of the look. You may even recall that the late Princess Diana was wearing one of these Peruvian designs in a photo widely released upon her engagement (but that was a long time ago, and I'm showing my age by sharing that story with you)!

INSTRUCTIONS FOR
PERUVIAN TURTLENECK SWEATER

BACK

Using color 1, cast on 42 (52, 62) sts. For size medium, work in 2 x 2 rib (k2, p2 every row) for 1" (3 cm). For sizes small and large, work as follows for 1" (3 cm):

Row 1 (RS): *K2, p2, rep from * across row, k2.

Row 2 (WS): *P2, k2, rep from * across row, p2.

Change to St st and work charts as follows, maintaining 1 edge stitch in color 1 at the beginning and end of each row.

Small: Work two widthwise repeats of Body chart (40 sts) as follows: Rows 1–28, rows 5–26. Work 3 rows Color 4, 1 row Color 5. You have worked 54 pattern rows.

Medium: Work 4 two-and-one-half widthwise repeats of Body chart (50 sts) as follows: Rows 1–28, rows 5–28, rows 5–26. Work 3 rows Color 4, 1 row Color 5. You have worked 78 pattern rows.

Large: Work three width-wise repeats of Body chart (60 sts) as follows: Rows 1–28, rows 5–28 three times. Work rows 1–12 of Stripe chart. You have worked 114 pattern rows.

For turtleneck, follow Stripe chart and work in 2 x 2 rib as for beginning for 4" (10 cm). Bind off in rib.

CHEST

Using color 1 cast on 22 (32, 42) sts. For size medium, work in 2 x 2 rib (k2, p2 every row) for 1" (3 cm). For sizes small and large, work as follows for 1" (3 cm):

Row 1 (RS): *K2, p2, rep from * across row, k2.

Row 2 (WS): *P2, k2, rep from * across row, p2.

Change to St st and work charts as follows, maintaining 1 edge stitch in color 1 at the beginning and end of each row. At the same time, when you have completed 34 (52, 76) pattern rows, decrease 1 st (k2tog) at the beginning and end of every knit row until 2 sts remain. Cut yarn leaving a tail for sewing and pull through last 2 sts to fasten off.

Small: Work one repeat of Body chart (20 sts) as follows: Rows 1–28. Work 7 sts color 1, work one-half repeat of Body chart (10 sts) Rows 5–26, work 7 sts color 1. Work 3 rows color 4, 1 row color 5. You have worked 54 pattern rows.

Medium: Work one-and-one-half repeats of Body chart (30 sts) as follows: Rows 1–28, rows 5–28. Work 5 sts color 1, one repeat of Body chart (20 sts) rows rows 5–26, work 5 sts color 1. Work 3 rows color 4, 1 row color 5. You have worked 78 pattern rows.

Large: Work two repeats of Body chart (40 sts) as follows: Rows 1–28, rows 5–28 two times. Work 11 sts color 1, one repeat of Body chart (20 sts) Rows 1–28, 11 sts color 1. Work rows 1–12 of Stripe chart. You have worked 114 pattern rows.

SLEEVES

Using color 1, cast on 28 (36, 44) sts. Work in 2 x 2 rib (k2, p2 every row) for 1" (3 cm).

Change to St st and work Stripe chart rows 1–24.

Finishing

For back piece, use length of yarn to sew together turtleneck of sweater. Leave yarn connected at bottom edge of turtleneck. Fit point of chest piece under seam at bottom of neck and stitch both sides of the triangle to the adjoining sides of the back of the sweater. Sew the remaining side seams from the bottom up, leaving an opening of 3 (4, 5)" (8 [10, 13] cm) for sleeve holes. Sew sleeves to leg holes. Weave in any loose ends with yarn needle.

MATERIALS

1 (2, 2) skeins worsted-weight yarn, Mission Falls 1824 Wool (100% superwash wool; 1.75 oz [50 g]/85 yds [78 m] in each of the following colors: 1. earth (brown), 2. sprout (yellow), 3. rhubarb (pink) 4. aster (blue), 5. squash (orange), or desired colors

US size 7 (4.5 mm) straight needles, or size to obtain gauge

Yarn needle

Pattern charts (page 121)

Finished Dimensions

Directions are for sizes small (medium, large).

Back: length 10 (14, 20)" (25 [36, 51] cm). 4" (10 cm) turtleneck, width 9 (12, 14) " (23 [30, 36] cm)

Chest: width 5 (7, 9)" (13 [18, 23] cm)

Circumference: 14 (18, 22)" (36 [46, 56] cm)

Gauge: 4.5 sts and 6 rows = 1" (3 cm) in stockinette stitch

4" × 4" (10 × 10 cm) swatch = 18 sts and 24 rows

space-yarn turtleneck sweater

This design is the perfect example of letting the yarn work for you. Some of today's modern yarns are spun with fibers, colors, and textures that vary as you go along, creating the most exciting results with no extra effort. You simply knit and purl to beautiful effect! I liked this sweater so much that I made one for myself, minus the turtleneck. (The pattern appears on page 114 and a photo of the space-yarn version appears on page 13.) You are the beneficiary of my efforts, and the matching people design is unisex, so it can be made for anyone you choose. Just beware of the "boyfriend sweater curse." It is said that if you knit a sweater for your boyfriend, you will have broken up by the time it is finished! (So, maybe that explains why mine didn't get his for Christmas.)

INSTRUCTIONS FOR
SPACE-YARN TURTLENECK SWEATER

BACK

Cast on 26 (34, 42) sts. Work as follows for 1" (3 cm):

Row 1 (RS): *K2, p2, rep from * across row, k2.

Row 2 (WS): *P2, k2, rep from * across row, p2.

Change to St st and work until piece measures 10 (14, 20)" (25 [36, 51] cm) to form body of sweater, ending in a purl row. Next row: work as follows for 4" (10 cm) to form turtleneck of sweater:

Row 1 (RS): *K2, p2, rep from * across row, k2.

Row 2 (WS): *P2, k2, rep from * across row, p2.

Bind off in rib pattern, leaving a length of yarn to be used to sew together the sweater.

CHEST

Cast on 16 (18, 24) sts. For sizes small and large, work in 2 × 2 rib (k2, p2 every row) for 1" (3 cm). For size medium, work as follows for 1" (3 cm):

Row 1 (RS): *K2, p2, rep from * across row, k2.

Row 2 (WS): *P2, k2, rep from * across row, p2.

Change to St st and work for 2 (3, 5)" (5 [8, 13] cm). Continue in St st, decreasing 1 st (k2tog) at beg and end of each following knit row until 1 st remains on needle. Cut and pull end of yarn through the stitch to fasten off work at point of triangle, leaving a length of yarn attached to chest plate to be used to sew together the chest of sweater.

Finishing

For back piece, use length of yarn to sew together turtleneck of sweater. Leave yarn connected at bottom edge of turtleneck. Fit point of chest piece under seam at bottom of neck and stitch both sides of the triangle to the adjoining sides of the back of the sweater. Sew the ribbed portion of the chest plate to the corresponding sides of the sweater, leaving two openings at the straight sides of the chest plate to form the leg holes (sleeve openings). Weave in any loose ends with yarn needle.

MATERIALS

1 skein bulky weight yarn, Plymouth Yarn Outback Wool (100% virgin wool; 7 oz [200 g]/370 yd [338 m]) in color 995 or desired color. Can also be made using Kraemer Yarns Mauch Chunky (100% wool; 3.5 oz [100 g]/120 yd [110 m]) in desired color

US size 11 (8 mm) straight needles or size to obtain gauge

Yarn needle

Finished Dimensions

Directions are for sizes small (medium, large).

Back: length 10 (14, 20)" (25 [36, 51] cm), 4" (10 cm) turtleneck, width 9 (12, 14)" (23 [30, 36] cm)

Chest: width 5 (6, 8)" (13 [15, 20] cm)

Circumference: 14 (18, 22)" (36 [46, 56] cm)

Gauge: 3 sts and 4 rows = 1" (3 cm) in stockinette stitch

4" × 4" (10 × 10 cm) swatch = 12 sts and 16 rows

Chapter Four

canine couture

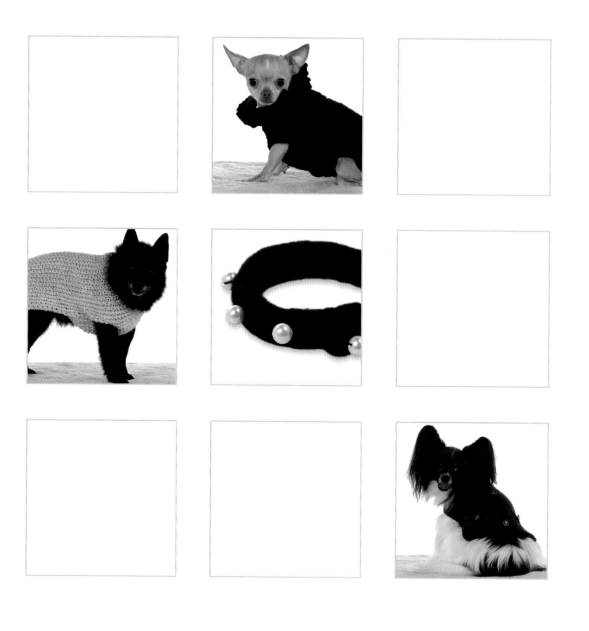

canine couture

Our dogs deserve a **touch of luxury** as much as we do. Indulge your pet by knitting him a stylish sweater inspired by the work of a famous designer. These couture creations are the height of chic and will surely identify our canine as a fashion leader!

"kennel" tweed cardigan jacket

You are familiar with "Koko Kennel," the French pet couturiere? Well, if not, it's high time you learned all about her. She reduced elegance to a simple formula: the little black dress, ropes of pearls, and the cardigan jacket trimmed with braid and brass buttons. Anyone who is anyone wears one. Now your pet can, too!

INSTRUCTIONS FOR
TWEED CARDIGAN JACKET

BACK

Starting at hem edge, cast on 36 (48, 56) sts. Using CC, work in seed stitch as follows for ½" (1 cm) to form contrast trim at hem:

Row 1: K1, p1, repeat across row.

Row 2: P1, k1, repeat across row.

Change to MC and continue in seed stitch pattern for 9½ (13½, 19½)" (24 [34, 50] cm) to form body of sweater.

Bind off in seed stitch, leaving a length of yarn attached to be used to sew together the sweater.

CONTRAST TRIM FOR BUTTON PLACKET AND POCKETS

Button Placket

Using CC, cast on 40 (56, 80) sts. Work in seed stitch for ½" (1 cm) and bind off.

Pocket Trim (make 4)

Using CC, cast on 8 (12, 16) sts. Work in seed stitch for ½" (1 cm) and bind off.

CHEST

▶ Starting at hem edge, cast on 20 (24, 32) sts. Work in seed stitch for 3 (4, 5)" (8 [10, 13] cm).

▶ Continue to work in seed stitch pattern, but decrease 1 st (k2tog) at beg and end of every RS row (every other row) until 1 st remains on the needle. Cut and pull yarn through remaining loop to fasten at point of triangle.

Finishing

Starting at the neck end of the back, use the attached length of yarn to sew together the top corners of the work to form the neck of the sweater. Do not cut the loose end of yarn when you are done. It will be used to sew the chest to the back of the sweater. Fit the triangular portion of the chest piece under the neck and use the remaining yarn to sew one side of the triangular form to the adjoining stockinette stitch portion of the back piece. Fasten yarn here securely and conceal end by pulling needle through a few stitches at the reverse side of the garment. Cut yarn.

Use the length of yarn at the top of the triangle to sew the other triangular

portion of the chest to the back. Conceal end of yarn as described previously and cut off. Thread a length of matching yarn through your needle and sew the bottom 2 (2, 3)" (5 [5, 8] cm) of the chest piece to the adjoining sides of the back piece at each side, making the chest piece lie flat against the back portion of the sweater. This will leave two openings, one at each side, to accommodate the dog's legs (armholes).

Sew the buttonhole placket to the center back of the sweater. Sew three ¹/₂" (1 cm) -diameter gold buttons to the placket. Place first button at the top of the placket, the next one at the center of the placket, and the third at the bottom of the placket. Sew the four

pocket trim pieces into place 2 (3, 6)" (5 [8, 15] cm) from the top and bottom of the sweater, ending 1 (1¹/₂, 2)" (3 [4, 5] cm) from the center placket. Sew a ¹/₂" (1 cm) -diameter gold button to the center of each pocket trim piece. Weave in any loose ends with yarn needle.

If you wish, you may use a crochet hook to attach a new length of yarn ¹/₂ (³/₄, 1)" (1 [2, 3] cm) from the center of the hem. Chain a length about 1 (1¹/₂, 2)" (3 [4, 5] cm) long and attach other end at the point ¹/₂" (1 cm) from the center on the other side. This will create a loop through which you can pull the dog's tail to secure the sweater to your pet at the hem of the garment.

MATERIALS

- 1 (1, 2) skein(s) main color (MC) and 1 (1, 1) skein contrast color (CC) worsted-weight yarn, Kraemer Yarns Summit Hill (100% merino superwash wool; 3.5 oz [100 g]/230 yds [210 m]) in ruby (MC) and obsidian (CC) or desired colors

- US size 9 (5.5 mm) straight needles or size to obtain gauge

- Seven ¹/₂" (1 cm) -diameter gold buttons

- Yarn needle

- Crochet hook (optional)

Finished Dimensions

Directions are for sizes small (medium, large).

Back: length 10 (14, 20)" (25 [36, 51] cm), width 9 (12, 14)" (23 [30, 36] cm)

Chest: width 5 (6, 8)" (13 [15, 20] cm)

Circumference: 14 (18, 22)" (36 [46, 56] cm)

Gauge: 4 sts and 6 rows = 1" (3 cm) in stockinette stitch

4" × 4" (10 × 10 cm) swatch = 16 sts and 24 rows

"canine klein" minimal design sweater

Another legendary designer has created a look especially for you. "Canine Klein" is known for his simplicity of line and form. It's all in the fit. Less is more, and in this sweater, your pet is the most!

INSTRUCTIONS FOR
MINIMAL DESIGN SWEATER

BACK

Using two strands of the yarn held together and starting at hem edge, cast on 26 (34, 42) sts. Work in seed stitch as follows for 10 (14, 20)" (25 [36, 51] cm).

Row 1: K1, p1, repeat across row.

Row 2: P1, k1, repeat across row.

Bind off in seed stitch, leaving a length of yarn to be used to sew together the sweater.

CHEST

Cast on 16 (18, 24) sts. Work in seed stitch as follows for 1 (2, 3)" (3 [5, 8] cm):

Row 1: K1, p1, repeat across row.

Row 2: P1, k1, repeat across row.

Continue in seed stitch and decrease 1 st (k2tog) at beg and end of each RS row (row 1) until 1 st remains on needle. Cut and pull end of yarn through the stitch to fasten off work at point of triangle. Cut off remaining yarn, leaving a length attached to chest plate to be used to sew together the chest of sweater.

Finishing

For back piece, use length of yarn to sew together the first and last stitches of the neck end of sweater. Leave yarn connected at neck. Fit point of chest piece under seam at bottom of neck and stitch both sides of the triangle to the adjoining sides of the back of the sweater. Sew the bottom 2 (2, 3)" (5 [5, 8] cm) portion of each side of the chest plate to the corresponding sides of the sweater, leaving two openings at the straight sides of the chest plate to form the leg holes (sleeve openings). Weave in any loose ends with yarn needle.

If you wish, you may use a crochet hook to attach a new length of two strands of yarn 1/2 (3/4, 1)" (1 [2, 3] cm) from the center of the hem. Chain a length about 1 (1 1/2, 2)" (3 [4, 5] cm) long and attach the other end of the chain 1/2 (3/4, 1)" (1 [2, 3] cm) from the center hem at the other side. This will create a loop through which you can pull the dog's tail to secure the sweater to your pet at the hem of the garment.

MATERIALS

2 (2, 4) skeins bulky weight yarn, Kraemer Yarns Summit Hill (100% merino superwash wool; 3.5 oz [100 g]/230 yds [210 m]) was used with two strands held together in natural or desired color

US size 11 (8 mm) straight needles or size to obtain gauge

Yarn needle

Crochet hook (optional)

Finished Dimensions

Directions are for sizes small (medium, large).

Back: length 10 (14, 20)" (25 [36, 51] cm), width 9 (12, 14)" (23 [30, 36] cm)

Chest: width 5 (6, 8)" (13 [15, 20] cm)

Circumference: 14 (18, 22)" (36 [46, 56] cm)

Gauge: 3 sts and 4 rows = 1" (3 cm) in stockinette stitch

4" × 4" (10 × 10 cm) swatch = 12 sts and 16 rows

"oscar de la rawhide" ruffled sweater

"Oscar de la Rawhide," known for his opulent eveningwear, created a look exclusively for this book. Here is an ultrafeminine, yet sophisticated, design. Ruffles frame your chien's lovely face and flounces form at the hem. When worn with the Felted Dog Collar, trimmed with pearls (see page 90), your pet will make a red-carpet entrance!

INSTRUCTIONS FOR
RUFFLED SWEATER

BACK

Using two strands of yarn held together, cast on 104 (136, 168) sts.

Row 1: K across row.

Row 2: P across row.

Row 3: K2tog across the entire row; 52 (68, 84) sts remain on needle.

Row 4: P across row.

Row 5: K2tog across the entire row; 26 (34, 42) sts remain on needle.

Continue to work evenly in St st until piece measures 10 (14, 20)" (25 [36, 51] cm), ending with a purl row. Next row: K into the front and back of each stitch in the row (k1f&b), resulting in 52 (68, 84) sts on the needle. Next row: Purl. Next row: K1f&b, resulting in 104 (136, 168) sts. Bind off in purl stitch.

CHEST

Cast on 16 (18, 24) sts. Work in 1 × 1 rib (k1, p1 every row) for 2" (5 cm). Change to St st and work for 1 (2, 3)" (3 [5, 8] cm). Continue in St st, decreasing 1 st at beg and end of each following knit row until 1 st remains on needle. Cut and pull end of yarn through the stitch to fasten off work at point of triangle. Cut off remaining yarn, leaving a length attached to chest plate to be used to sew together the chest of sweater.

Finishing

For back piece, use length of yarn to sew together ruffled neckline of sweater. Leave yarn connected at bottom edge of ruffled neckline. Fit point of chest piece under seam at bottom of neckline and stitch both sides of the triangle to the adjoining sides of the back of the sweater. Sew the ribbed portion of the chest plate to the corresponding sides of the sweater, leaving two openings at the straight sides of the chest plate to form the leg holes (sleeve openings). Weave in any loose ends with yarn needle.

MATERIALS

1 (1, 2) skein(s) bulky weight yarn, Kraemer Yarns Summit Hill (100% merino superwash wool; 3.5 oz [100 g]/230 yd [210 m]) in obsidian or desired color. Knit holding two strands together to create the bulky weight

US size 11 (8 mm) straight needles

Yarn needle

Finished Dimensions

Directions are for sizes small (medium, large).

Back: length 10 (14, 20)" (25 [36, 51] cm), width 9 (12, 14)" (23 [30, 36] cm)

Chest: width 5 (6, 8)" (13 [15, 20] cm)

Circumference: 14 (18, 22)" (36 [46, 56] cm)

Gauge: 3 sts and 4 rows = 1" (3 cm) in stockinette stitch

4" × 4" (10 × 10 cm) swatch = 12 sts and 16 rows

felted dog collar

This collar is a fashionable addition to almost any sweater in this book. It can be knit from any wool fiber yarn that has not been treated with a superwash process. It is strictly decorative, and it is not meant to be used with a leash to walk your pet. If you want it to be functional, simply sew the decorative collar onto a store-bought one.

INSTRUCTIONS FOR
FELTED DOG COLLAR

COLLAR

- ▶ Take two double-pointed needles from the set and, using two strands of yarn, cast 7 stitches onto one of them. Do not turn work, but slide stitches back to the other side of the needle (using the I-cord method).

- ▶ Taking the yarn firmly across the back of work, k7. Slide stitches back to other side of needle.

- ▶ Repeat until strap measures 20" (51 cm) and bind off. Weave in any loose ends with yarn needle.

FELTING

Refer to general felting instructions on page 19. The machine-washing technique is recommended if you are also making the felted tote bag (see page 42) at the same time, as it uses a lot of water and energy and may be excessive for only a small collar.

Given this project's small size, felting by hand is a suitable option. Place the collar into a basin or bucket filled with hot water to which you have added a small amount of laundry detergent. You should wear rubber gloves to protect your hands from the hot water. Gently rub and agitate the collar under the hot water and continue until it has shrunken to the desired size. Rinse and let dry.

TRIM

This collar can be knit to match any sweater that is made with Mauch Chunky in this book. We are showing a black pearls design. For this design, stitch an assortment of faux pearls onto the finished collar in an appealing manner. Sew a small piece of Velcro to the underside of the end of the collar and sew the corresponding piece of fuzzy fabric to the top of the other end of the collar, overlapping about 1½" (4 cm) on each side. This finished collar will fit a dog who wears a size 12 collar. Adjust the length of your original knitting, and shrinking, to fit your own pet's neck.

MATERIALS

1 skein bulky weight yarn, Kraemer Yarns Mauch Chunky (100% wool; 3.5 oz [100 g]/120 yd [110 m]) in black or desired color. You may knit this collar using yarn left over from other projects you have knit from this book

US size 13 (9 mm) double-pointed needles

Yarn needle

Finished Dimensions

You can knit this collar smaller or larger to accommodate the neck measurement of your pet.

As originally knit: length 20" (51 cm)

After washing and felting: length: 15" (38 cm), to fit a dog whose neck measures 12"–14" (30–36 cm).

Gauge: 4 sts = 1" in stockinette stitch

Chapter Five

textured tales

textured tales

Texture is a wonderful design element. It is created by a patterned stitch, or by special yarns, which have lumps, loops, slubs, or other surface interests. These yarns create the texture by themselves, without the need to knit the sweater in a special pattern stitch. What could be easier?

contrast turtleneck sweater

Try this sporty and casual look on a cold afternoon. You can knit this design in muted or bright colors for different effects. Or, pair a muted tone with a bright one for a shot of color as shown here.

INSTRUCTIONS FOR
CONTRAST TURTLENECK SWEATER

BACK

Using CC and starting at hem edge, cast on 26 (34, 42) sts. Work as follows for 1" (3 cm):

Row 1 (RS): *K2, p2, rep from * across row, k2.

Row 2 (WS): *P2, k2, rep from * across row, p2.

Change to MC and work in St st until piece measures 10 (14, 20)" (25 [36, 51] cm) to form body of sweater, ending in a purl row. Next row, using CC, work as follows for 4" (10 cm) to form turtleneck of sweater:

Row 1 (RS): *K2, p2, rep from * across row, k2.

Row 2 (WS): *P2, k2, rep from * across row, p2.

Bind off in rib pattern, leaving a length of yarn to be used to sew together the sweater.

CHEST

Using CC, cast on 16 (18, 24) sts. For sizes small and large, work in 2 × 2 rib (k2, p2 every row) for 1" (3 cm). For size medium, work as follows for 1" (3 cm):

Row 1 (RS): *K2, p2, rep from * across row, k2.

Row 2 (WS): *P2, k2, rep from * across row, p2.

Change to MC and work in St st for 2 (3, 5)" (5 [8, 13] cm). Continue in St st, decreasing 1 st (k2tog) at beg and end of each following knit row until 1 st remains on needle. Cut and pull end of yarn through the stitch to fasten off work at point of triangle, leaving a length of yarn attached to chest plate to be used to sew together the chest of sweater.

Finishing

For back piece, use length of yarn to sew together turtleneck of sweater. Leave yarn connected at bottom edge of turtleneck. Fit point of chest piece under seam at bottom of neck and stitch both sides of the triangle to the adjoining sides of the back of the sweater. Sew the ribbed portion of the chest plate to the corresponding sides of the sweater, leaving two openings at the straight sides of the chest plate to form the leg holes (sleeve openings). Weave in any loose ends with yarn needle.

MATERIALS

- 1 skein main color (MC) and 1 skein contrast color (CC) bulky weight yarn, Kraemer Yarns Mauch Chunky (100% wool; 3.5 oz [100 g]/120 yd [110 m]) in walnut (MC) and pumpkin (CC) or desired colors
- US size 11 (8 mm) straight needles or size to obtain gauge
- Yarn needle

Finished Dimensions

Directions are for sizes small (medium, large).

Back: length 10 (14, 20)" (25 [36, 51] cm), 4" (10 cm) turtleneck, width 9 (12, 14)" (23 [30, 36] cm)

Chest: width 5 (6, 8)" (13 [15, 20] cm)

Circumference: 14 (18, 22)" (36 [46, 56] cm)

Gauge: 3 sts and 4 rows = 1" (3 cm) in stockinette stitch

4" × 4" (10 × 10 cm) swatch = 12 sts and 16 rows

bulky knit turtleneck sweater

This pattern knits up in a flash! Use bulky yarns, or pair two thinner, contrasting yarns together for a tweedy effect. The heavy weight of this design makes it a warm choice for those cold winter days; your dog is sure to thank you.

INSTRUCTIONS FOR
BULKY KNIT TURTLENECK SWEATER

BACK

Cast on 26 (34, 42) sts. Work as follows for 1" (3 cm):

Row 1 (RS): *K2, p2, rep from * across row, k2.

Row 2 (WS): *P2, k2, rep from * across row, p2.

Change to St st and work until piece measures 10 (14, 20)" (25 [36, 51] cm) to form body of sweater, ending in a purl row. Next row: work as follows for 4" (10 cm) to form turtleneck of sweater:

Row 1 (RS): *K2, p2, rep from * across row, k2.

Row 2 (WS): *P2, k2, rep from * across row, p2.

Bind off in rib pattern, leaving a length of yarn to be used to sew together the sweater.

CHEST

Cast on 16 (18, 24) sts. For sizes small and large, work in 2 × 2 rib (k2, p2 every row) for 1" (3 cm). For size medium, work as follows for 1" (3 cm):

Row 1 (RS): *K2, p2, rep from * across row, k2.

Row 2 (WS): *P2, k2, rep from * across row, p2.

Change to St st and work for 2 (3, 5)" (5 [8, 13] cm). Continue in St st, decreasing 1 st (k2tog) at beg and end of each following knit row until 1 st remains on needle. Cut and pull end of yarn through the stitch to fasten off work at point of triangle, leaving a length of yarn attached to chest plate to be used to sew together the chest of sweater.

Finishing

For back piece, use length of yarn to sew together turtleneck of sweater. Leave yarn connected at bottom edge of turtleneck. Fit point of chest piece under seam at bottom of neck and stitch both sides of the triangle to the adjoining sides of the back of the sweater. Sew the ribbed portion of the chest plate to the corresponding sides of the sweater, leaving two openings at the straight sides of the chest plate to form the leg holes (sleeve openings). Weave in any loose ends with yarn needle.

MATERIALS

1 skein bulky weight yarn, Kraemer Yarns Mauch Chunky (100% wool; 3.5 oz [100 g]/120 yds [110 m]) in desired color

US size 11 (8 mm) straight needles or size to obtain gauge

Yarn needle

Finished Dimensions

Directions are for sizes small (medium, large).

Back: length 10 (14, 20)" (25 [36, 51] cm), 4" (10 cm) turtleneck, width 9 (12, 14)" (23 [30, 36] cm)

Chest: width 5 (6, 8)" (13 [15, 20] cm)

Circumference: 14 (18, 22)" (36 [46, 56] cm)

Gauge: 3 sts and 4 rows = 1" (3 cm) in stockinette stitch

4" × 4" (10 × 10 cm) swatch = 12 sts and 16 rows

chunky knit turtleneck sweater

This basic design reflects your personal style through your choice of yarn and colors. This is another example of a yarn doing all the work. This sweater, and the matching women's V-Neck Pullover Vest (see page 102), is knit with a yarn imported from Japan. Noro yarns are space-dyed and change colors in a regular sequence. They have interesting texture, and they are made of unique fiber blends. Any of their bulky weight yarns is suitable for this design; simply check your gauge for accurate results. You can use Kraemer yarns for this sweater; I recommend Mauch Chunky for its softness and unique textural interest.

INSTRUCTIONS FOR CHUNKY KNIT TURTLENECK SWEATER

BACK

Cast on 26 (34, 42) stitches. Work as follows for 1" (3 cm):

Row 1 (RS): *K2, p2, rep from * across row, k2.

Row 2 (WS): *P2, k2, rep from * across row, p2.

Change to St st and work until piece measures 10 (14, 20)" (25 [36, 51] cm) to form body of sweater, ending in a purl row. Next row: work as follows for 4" (10 cm) to form turtleneck of sweater:

Row 1 (RS): *K2, p2, rep from * across row, k2.

Row 2 (WS): *P2, k2, rep from * across row, p2.

Bind off in rib pattern, leaving a length of yarn to be used to sew together the sweater.

CHEST

Cast on 16 (18, 24) sts. For sizes small and large, work in 2 × 2 rib (k2, p2 every row) for 1" (3 cm). For size medium, work as follows for 1" (3 cm):

Row 1 (RS): *K2, p2, rep from * across row, k2.

Row 2 (WS): *P2, k2, rep from * across row, p2.

Change to St st and work for 2 (3, 5)" (5 [8, 13] cm). Continue in St st, decreasing 1 st (k2tog) at beg and end of each following knit row until 1 st remains on needle. Cut and pull end of yarn through the stitch to fasten off work at point of triangle, leaving a length of yarn attached to chest plate to be used to sew together the chest of sweater.

Finishing

For back piece, use length of yarn to sew together turtleneck of sweater. Leave yarn connected at bottom edge of turtleneck. Fit point of chest piece under seam at bottom of neck and stitch both sides of the triangle to the adjoining sides of the back of the sweater. Sew the ribbed portion of the chest plate to the corresponding sides of the sweater, leaving two openings at the straight sides of the chest plate to form the leg holes (sleeve openings). Weave in any loose ends with yarn needle.

MATERIALS

1 (1, 2) skein(s) bulky weight yarn, Noro yarn, Kureyon (100% wool; 1.76 oz [50 g]/110 yds [100 m]), a space-dyed yarn was used in the sample shown in color #150, but it comes in 24 color combinations. Can also use Kraemer Yarns Mauch Chunky (100% wool; 3.5 oz [100 g]/120 yd [110 m]) in desired color

US size 11 (8 mm) straight needles or size to obtain gauge

Yarn needle

Finished Dimensions

Directions are for sizes small (medium, large).

Back: length 10 (14, 20)" (25 [36, 51] cm), 4" (10 cm) turtleneck, width 9 (12, 14)" (23 [30, 36] cm)

Chest: width 5 (6, 8)" (13 [15, 20] cm)

Circumference: 14 (18, 22)" (36 [46, 56] cm)

Gauge: 3 sts and 4 rows = 1" (3 cm) in stockinette stitch

4" × 4" (10 × 10 cm) swatch = 12 sts and 16 rows

v-neck pullover vest

This human-sized vest is knit short, boxy, and oversized. Knit it in a smaller size for a more fitted appearance, or knit it longer in order for it to hit at the hip, instead of slightly below the waist, as shown in the sample.

INSTRUCTIONS FOR
V-NECK
PULLOVER VEST

BACK

▶ Cast on 54 (56, 58) sts. Work in either 1 × 1 rib or 2 × 2 rib, according to your preference, for 1" (3 cm) or 2" (5 cm), according to your preference, ending with a WS row. The 1 × 1 rib will result in a slightly tighter hem fit. A 1" (3 cm) ribbing will result in a looser fitting hem, while the 2" (5 cm) ribbing will produce a more classic fitted hemline.

▶ Change to St st and work for 12" (30 cm) (fit to slightly below the waist) or longer (desired length to underarm), ending with a purl row.

- Continue in St st and bind off 4 sts at beg of next two rows. Continue in St st, decreasing 1 st (k2tog) at each end of following knit rows, three times until 40 (42, 44) sts remain.

- Work even in St st until armhole measures 7 (7½, 8)" (18 [19, 20] cm). Bind off 6 sts at beg of next two rows, then 6 (7, 7) sts at beg of next two rows until 16 (16, 18) sts remain. Bind off remaining stitches loosely for back of neck.

FRONT

- Cast on 54 (56, 58) sts. Work as for back until after decreases for armholes, when 40 (42, 44) sts remain, ending with a purl row.

- Next row, k25 (26, 27) sts, then k2tog. This will form the center of the v-neck.

- Attach another ball of yarn and k2tog, then knit across the rest of the row. Next row, purl across the first half of the front and, using the yarn from the other ball of yarn, continue to purl across the remaining half of the row. Both sides of the v-neck will be worked at once from the two different balls of yarn.

- *Next row, knit across stitches until two remain on needle, then k2tog. Using other ball of yarn, k2tog and knit across rest of row. Next row, purl evenly across both sides of neckline.* Continue to follow these two rows (from * to *) until 6 (7, 7) sts remain on needle on each side of the v-neckline.

- Continue to knit evenly in St st until front armhole matches length of back armhole, ending with a purl row. Bind off 6 (7, 7) sts on each side of neckline on the next knit row.

Finishing

Sew front shoulders to back shoulders. Sew side seams. Crochet one row of single crochet around each sleeve opening and around v-neckline.

Optional neckline finishing is to pick up 60 sts evenly around neckline opening on circular or double-pointed needles. Place a marker at the center of the v-neck. Beginning at the center of the v-neckline, knit one row of 1 × 1 rib (k1, p1 every row) around the entire neckline. Next row, k2tog at beginning of v-neckline and work in 1 × 1 rib evenly around the neckline until you reach the last two stitches in front of the marker. K these 2 sts tog. Continue in this manner, decreasing 2 sts each round at the center front of the v-neckline, and continuing the rib pattern, until ribbed binding measures 1" (3 cm). Bind off in 1 × 1 rib. Weave in any loose ends with yarn needle.

MATERIALS

Sizes small (6–8), medium (10–12), and large (14–16).

4 skeins bulky weight yarn, Noro yarn, Kureyon (100% wool; 1.76 oz [50 g]/110 yd [100 m]), a space-dyed yarn was used in the sample shown in color #150, but it comes in 24 color combinations. Can also use Kraemer Yarns Mauch Chunky (100% wool; 3.5 oz [100 g]/120 yd [110 m]) or Kraemer Yarns Naturally Nazareth (100% wool; 3.5 oz [100 g]/184 yd [168 m]). If using Kraemer Yarns Summit Hill (100% merino superwash wool; 3.5 oz [100 g]/230 yd [210 m]) or Kraemer Yarns Tatamy Tweed (45% cotton, 55% acrylic; 3.5 oz [100 g]/250 yd [229 m]), hold two strands together

US size 11 (8 mm) straight needles or size to obtain gauge

Size K crochet hook

Yarn needle

Finished Dimensions

Directions are for sizes small (medium, large): 6–8 (10–12, 14–16); approx. 36 (38, 40)" (90 [95, 100] cm) in circumference

Gauge: 3 sts and 4 rows = approx. 1" (3 cm)

knit the knots
mixed-ball sweater

This design is sometimes called a Mystery Ball sweater, and it is a great way to use up your yarn stash! Simply pull out all your leftover yarn, even what you have in tiny quantities. Arrange it by color story, combining all shades of one color, or knit a multicolored rainbow.

There are two methods for knitting this sweater. Method one involves taking random lengths of assorted yarns and tying them together with knots. Wind the ball as you go, and when you have enough (when it looks like a commercially packaged ball of yarn), knit it into the sweater. The other method involves knitting and tying as you go, changing and knotting yarns at your whim. You'll need to maintain a relatively consistent yarn diameter to keep your gauge accurate. Do this by "plying" the thinner yarns, or, in other words, put several strands of thinner yarns together to make a bulkier strand. Either method will create a one-of-a-kind look that both you and your pet will love!

(continued on page 106)

MATERIALS

Use chunky weight yarns, tied together in random lengths, with the knots at the back of the work. If you wish, knit a gauge swatch, and adjust the number of stitches to reflect a gauge that may differ from the one given here. I have listed the yarns used in my sample below:

- 1 skein Kraemer Yarns Mauch Chunky (100% wool; 3.5 oz [100 g]/120 yd [110 m]) in strawberry, single strand
- 1 skein Tatamy Tweed (45% cotton, 55% acrylic; 3.5 oz [100 g]/250 yd [229 m]) in cherry, four strands held together
- 1 skein Lion Brand Yarns Fancy Fur (55% polyamide, 45% polyester; 1.75 oz [50 g]/39 yd [35 m]) in rainbow red, held with one strand of Mauch Chunky in strawberry
- 1 skein Lion Brand Yarns Fun Fur (100% polyester; solids:1.75 oz [50 g]/60 yd [54 m]; prints: 1.5 oz [40 g]/57 yd [52 m]) in red, held with one strand of Mauch Chunky in strawberry
- 1 skein Lion Brand Yarns Chenille Thick & Quick (91% acrylic, 9% rayon; solids: 100 yd [90 m]; prints: 75 yd [68 m]) in scarlet, single strand
- 1 skein Bernat Ping Pong (73% acrylic, 27% nylon; 1.75 oz [50 g]/58 yd [53 m]) in red (color 51430), single strand
- 1 skein Red Heart Light and Lofty (100% acrylic; solids: 6 oz [170 g]/148 yd [135 m]; prints: 4.5 oz [128 g]/100 yd [91 m]) in wine, single strand
- 1 skein Patons Brilliant (69% acrylic, 31% polyester; 1.75 oz [50 g]/166 yd [152 m]) in radiant red, two strands held together
- 1 skein Caron Feathers (65% acrylic, 35% nylon; 1.75 oz [50 g]/70 yd [50 m]) in macaw (color 12), single strand
- US size 11 (8 mm) straight needles or size to obtain gauge
- Yarn needle

Gauge: 3 sts and 4 rows = 1" (3 cm) in stockinette stitch

4" × 4" (10 × 10 cm) swatch = 12 sts and 16 rows

Finished Dimensions

Directions are for sizes small (medium, large).

Back: length 10 (14, 20)" (25 [36, 51] cm), width 9 (12, 14)" (23 [30, 36] cm)

Chest: width 5 (6, 8)" (13 [15, 20] cm)

Circumference: 14 (18, 22)" (36 [46, 56] cm)

INSTRUCTIONS FOR
KNIT THE KNOTS
MIXED-BALL SWEATER

BACK

Starting at hem edge, cast on 26 (34, 42) sts. Work in 2 × 2 rib as follows for 1" (3 cm):

Row 1 (RS): *K2, p2, rep from * across row, k2.

Row 2 (WS): *P2, k2, rep from * across row, p2.

Change to St st and work until piece measures 10 (14, 20)" (25 [36, 51] cm) to form body of sweater. Bind off in knit stitch leaving a length of yarn to be used to sew together the sweater.

CHEST

Cast on 16 (18, 24) sts. For sizes small and large, work in 2 × 2 rib (k2, p2 every row) for 1" (3 cm). For size medium, work as follows for 1" (3 cm):

Row 1 (RS): *K2, p2, rep from * across row, k2.

Row 2 (WS): *P2, k2, rep from * across row, p2.

Change to St st and work for 2 (3, 5)" (5 [8, 13] cm). Continue in St st, decreasing 1 st (k2tog) at beg and end of each following knit row until 1 st remains on needle. Cut and pull end of yarn through the stitch to fasten off work at point of triangle, leaving a length of yarn attached to chest plate to be used to sew together the chest of sweater.

Finishing

For back piece, use length of yarn to sew together top corners to form neck of sweater. Leave yarn connected at bottom edge of neck. Fit point of chest piece under seam at bottom of neck and stitch both sides of the triangle to the adjoining sides of the back of the sweater. Sew the ribbed portion of the chest plate to the corresponding sides of the sweater, leaving two openings at the straight sides of the chest plate to form the leg holes (sleeve openings). Weave in any loose ends with yarn needle.

fisherman knit cardigan

This v-necked cardigan is knit in traditional Aran patterns. You can choose any button design that reflects your sense of style. If your pet has a tendency to chew on small objects, sew the front of the sweater closed, and embroider faux buttons to complete the look. This is the most complicated sweater in the book, best for experienced knitters.

STITCHES USED FOR FISHERMAN KNIT SWEATER

Twisted Sts
(multiple of 2)

Row 1: (RS) K2.

Row 2: (WS) P2.

Row 3: (RS) K2tog but leave on needle, then insert right-hand needle between the 2 sts just knitted together and knit the first st again, then slip both sts from needle.

Row 4: (WS) P2.

Repeat rows 1–4 for Twisted St pattern.

Astrakan St
(multiple of 4)

Row 1: (RS) P.

Row 2: (WS) *[(K1, p1, k1) into next stitch, p3tog], rep from *.

Row 3: (RS) P.

Row 4: (WS) *[P3tog, (k1, p1, k1) into next stitch], rep from *.

Repeat rows 1–4 for Astrakan St pattern.

Moss Variation St
(multiple of 4)

Row 1: (RS) K1, p1.

Row 2: (WS) K1, p1.

Row 3: (RS) P1, k1.

Row 4: (WS) P1, k1.

Repeat rows 1–4 for Moss Variation St pattern.

4-St Front Cable
(multiple of 4)

Row 1: (RS) Sl 1 to cn, hold in front, k3, k1 from cn.

Row 2: (WS) P.

Row 3: (RS) K.

Row 4: (WS) P.

Repeat rows 1–4 for Cable St pattern.

1x1 Rib (multiple of 2)

Row 1: (RS) K1, p1.

Row 2: (WS) P1, k1.

Repeat rows 1 and 2 for Rib St pat.

MATERIALS

- 1 skein worsted-weight yarn, Kraemer Yarns Summit Hill (100% merino superwash wool; 3.5 oz [100 g]/230 yd [210 m]) in pearl or desired color
- US size 9 (5.5 mm) straight needles or size to obtain gauge
- Three 1¼" (3 cm) buttons
- Five stitch holders
- Stitch markers
- Cable needle
- Yarn needle

Finished Dimensions

One size to fit small dogs.

Back: length 12" (30 cm), 1" (3 cm) stand-up neck, width 9½" (24 cm)

Chest: width 8" (20 cm)

Circumference: 17½" (44 cm)

Gauge: 4 sts and 6 rows = 1" (3 cm) in stockinette stitch

4" × 4" (10 × 10 cm) swatch = 16 sts and 24 rows

INSTRUCTIONS FOR
FISHERMAN KNIT SWEATER

BOTTOM FLAP

Cast on 38 sts. Beg k1, p1 rib. Work in rib for eight rows, ending with a WS row. Beg pats.

Row 1: (RS) *K1, p1, rep from * twice; over next 4 sts work row 1 of 4-St Front Cable; p1, k1, p14, k1, p1; over next 4 sts work row 1 of 4-St Front Cable, *p1, k1, rep from * twice.

Row 2: (WS) *P1, k1, rep from * twice; p4, k1, p1, k1, beg Astrakan St, [(k1, p1, k1) into next st, p3 tog], rep twice, k1, p1, k1, p4, *k1, p1, rep from * twice.

Row 3: (RS) *P1, k1, rep from * once, k1, p1, k4, p1, k1, p14, k1, p1, k4, p1, k1, *k1, p1, rep from * once.

Row 4: (WS) *K1, p1, rep from * once, p1, k1, p4, k1, p1, k1, [p3 tog, (k1, p1, k1) into next st] rep twice, k1, p1, k1, p4, k1, p1, *p1, k1 rep from * once.

Rep rows 1–4 until piece measures 3½" (9 cm), ending with a WS row.

CARDIGAN SIDES

Right front cast on (RS): Cast on 20 sts, place marker (pm), work remaining 38 sts in pats as established.

Left front cast on (WS): Cast on 20 sts, pm, work 38 sts in pats as established, work 1 × 1 rib over rem 20 sts—78 sts, total.

Next row (RS): Work 1 × 1 rib to marker, work center 38 sts as established to marker, work 1 × 1 rib on rem 20 sts. Cont in pats as established until right front has 1" (3 cm) of rib (left side will have one row less), ending with a WS row.

Buttonhole and beg pat Buttonhole Row 1: Work 2 rib sts, bind off 2 sts, work 2 rib sts, beg Moss Variation Row 1 to marker (14 sts in Moss Variation), work 38 sts as established, work 14 sts in Moss Variation, maintain rem 6 sts for left front edge in 1 × 1 rib.

Buttonhole Row 2: Work all pats as established to last 4 sts, cast on 2 sts, work last 2 sts in rib. Maintain 6 sts at each end in rib, cont in pats as established. Repeat buttonhole rows 1 and 2 at 2" (5 cm) intervals until 3 buttonholes are made. Work even until piece measures 9" (23 cm) from bottom of flap, ending with a WS row.

RAGLAN SHAPING–RIGHT FRONT

Next row: Work 15 sts, p2tog, work next 2 sts in row 1 of Twisted Sts, p1, place rem sts on holder.

Row 1 (WS): Work sts in pats as established.

Row 2 (RS): Work to last 5 sts, p2tog, work Twisted Sts, p1.

Rep rows 1 and 2, 11 times. Place rem 7 sts on holder.

RAGLAN SHAPING–BACK

Row 1 (RS): Working sts for back from holder, p1, work next 2 sts in row 1 of Twisted Sts, ssk, work in pat to last 5 sts, p2tog, work next 2 sts in row 1 of Twisted Sts, p1 (Note: 20 sts rem on holder to be worked later as left front).

Row 2 (WS): Work pats as established.

Rep rows 1 and 2, 11 times. Place rem 14 sts on holder.

RAGLAN SHAPING–LEFT FRONT

Reverse shaping of right front, substituting ssk for p2tog.

SLEEVES (make 2)

Cast on 20 sts. Beg 1 × 1 rib. Work 7 rows in rib.

Row 8 (WS): Inc 6 sts evenly across row—26 sts.

Next row: Beg Moss Variation. Work even in Moss Variation until piece measures 4" (10 cm).

Raglan Shaping Row 1 (RS): P1, work next 2 sts in row 1 of Twisted Sts, ssk, work in pat to last 5 sts, p2tog, work next 2 sts in row 1 of Twisted Sts, p1.

Row 2 (WS): Work sts as established.

Rep rows 1 and 2, 10 times. Work even two rows, place rem 4 sts on holder.

Finishing

Neck Rib: With RS facing, work in 1 × 1 rib. Work 7 sts from right front holder, 4 sts from one sleeve holder, 14 sts from back holder, 4 sts from second sleeve holder, and 7 sts from left front holder. Cont on 36 sts in 1 × 1 rib for 1". Bind off loosely in rib stitch. Sew on buttons. Weave in any loose ends with yarn needle.

kwik-knit shaggy sweater

This furry sweater takes its texture from the eyelash yarns, which are paired with a plain bulky yarn. The result is an exotic sweater that is sure to attract attention of the best kind. The resulting yarn is very thick—there are only two stitches to the inch. It knits up in no time at all!

INSTRUCTIONS FOR
KWIK KNIT SHAGGY SWEATER

BACK

Starting at hem edge, cast on 18 (24, 28) sts. For sizes medium and large, work in 2 × 2 rib (k2, p2 every row) for four rows. For size small, work as follows for four rows:

Row 1 (RS): *K2, p2, rep from * across row, k2.

Row 2 (WS): *P2, k2, rep from * across row, p2.

Change to St st and work until piece measures 10 (14, 20)" (25 [36, 51] cm) to form body of sweater. Bind off in knit stitch, leaving a length of yarn to be used to sew together the sweater.

CHEST

Cast on 10 (12, 16) sts. For sizes medium and large, work in 2 × 2 rib (k2, p2 every row) for 1" (3 cm). For size small, work as follows for 1" (3 cm):

Row 1 (RS): *K2, p2, rep from * across row, k2.

Row 2 (WS): *P2, k2, rep from * across row, p2.

Change to St st and work until piece measures 2 (3, 5)" (5 [8, 13] cm). Continue in St st, decreasing 1 st (k2tog) at beg and end of each following knit row until 1 st remains on needle. Cut and pull end of yarn through the stitch to fasten off work at point of triangle, leaving a length of yarn attached to chest plate to be used to sew together the chest of sweater.

Finishing

For back piece, use length of yarn to sew together top corners to form neck of sweater. Leave yarn connected at bottom edge of neck. Fit point of chest piece under seam at bottom of neck and stitch both sides of the triangle to the adjoining sides of

the back of the sweater. Sew the ribbed portion of the chest plate to the corresponding sides of the sweater, leaving two openings at the straight sides of the chest plate to form the leg holes (sleeve openings). Weave in any loose ends with yarn needle.

MATERIALS

1 skein bulky weight yarn, Kraemer Yarns Mauch Chunky (100% wool; 3.5 oz [100 g]/120 yd [110 m]) in strawberry or desired color; 1 skein Lion Brand Yarns Fancy Fur (55% polyamide, 45% polyester; 1.75 oz [50 g]/39 yd [35 m]) in rainbow red or desired color

US size 13 (9 mm) straight needles or size to obtain gauge

Yarn needle

Finished Dimensions

Directions are for sizes small (medium, large).

Back: length 10 (14, 20)" (25 [36, 51] cm), width 9 (12, 14)" (23 [30, 36] cm)

Chest: width 5 (6, 8)" (13 [15, 20] cm)

Circumference: 14 (18, 22)" (36 [46, 56] cm)

Gauge:

2 sts and 2 rows = 1" (3 cm) in stockinette stitch

4" × 4" (10 × 10 cm) swatch = 8 sts and 8 rows

bulky knit crewneck sweater

This sweater is one of the most versatile you will ever make. This crewneck and the matching people version, Unisex Crewneck Sweater for People on page 114, can be made in a multitude of different yarns, colors, and textures and no two will look alike. I have made these well-loved patterns over and over again for myself and for friends. The sweater can be knit a little tighter, a little looser, a little shorter, a little longer, and it looks different every time. This version is elegant, knit from gorgeous cashmere I had leftover from another project.

INSTRUCTIONS FOR
BULKY KNIT CREWNECK SWEATER

BACK

▶ Cast on 26 (34, 42) sts. Work in 1 × 1 (k1, p1 every row) rib for 2" (5 cm).

▶ Change to St st and work until piece measures 10 (14, 20)" (25 [36, 51] cm) to form body of sweater, ending in a purl row.

▶ Next row, change to 1 × 1 rib and work for 1" (3 cm) to form crewneck of sweater. Bind off in rib, leaving a length of yarn to be used to sew together the sweater.

CHEST

▶ Cast on 16 (18, 24) sts. Work in 1 × 1 (k1, p1 every row) rib for 1" (3 cm). Change to St st and work for 2 (3, 5)" (5 [8, 13] cm).

▶ Continue in St st, decreasing 1 st (k2tog) at beg and end of each following knit row until 1 st remains on needle. Cut and pull end of yarn through the stitch to fasten off work at point of triangle, leaving a length of yarn attached to chest plate to be used to sew together the chest of sweater.

Finishing

For back piece, use length of yarn to sew together crewneck of sweater. Leave yarn connected at bottom edge of crewneck. Fit point of chest piece under seam at bottom of neck and stitch both sides of the triangle to the adjoining sides of the back of the sweater. Sew the ribbed portion of the chest plate to the corresponding sides of the sweater, leaving two openings at the straight sides of the chest plate to form the leg holes (sleeve openings). Weave in any loose ends with yarn needle.

MATERIALS

- 1 skein Kraemer Yarns Mauch Chunky (100% wool; 3.5 oz [100 g]/120 yd [110 m]) in desired color.
- US size 11 (8 mm) straight needles or size to obtain gauge
- Yarn needle

Finished Dimensions

Directions are for sizes small (medium, large).

Back: length 10 (14, 20)" (25 [36, 51] cm), 1" (3 cm) crewneck, width 9 (12, 14)" (23 [30, 36] cm)

Chest: width 5 (6, 8)" (13 [15, 20] cm)

Circumference: 14 (18, 22)" (36 [46, 56] cm)

Gauge: 3 sts and 4 rows = 1" (3 cm) in stockinette stitch

4" × 4" (10 × 10 cm) swatch = 12 sts and 16 rows

unisex crewneck sweater for people

This sweater is designed to fit both women and men. The sweater has raglan sleeves, and is designed to fit like an oversized sweatshirt, with the hem at the hip. If you wish, it can be knit shorter so that the ribbed hem sits just below the waist. If you choose to knit the shorter version, subtract 3" (8 cm) from the length of the front and back pieces. (A modified dog sweater version of this project can be seen on page 112.)

INSTRUCTIONS FOR

UNISEX CREWNECK SWEATER

BACK

Using size 9 straight needles, cast on 50 (56, 62, 68) sts. For sizes medium and extra large, work in 2 × 2 rib (k2, p2 every row) for 2" (5 cm). For sizes small and large, work as follows for 2" (5 cm):

Row 1 (RS): *K2, p2, rep from * across row, k2.

Row 2 (WS): *P2, k2, rep from * across row, p2.

Change to size 11 straight needles and work even in St st until piece measures 15 (15, 15½, 15½)" (38 [38, 39, 39] cm), or desired length to underarm, ending in a purl row. Continue to work in St st to shape full-fashioned raglan armholes as follows:

At the beginning of the next two rows bind off 2 (2, 3, 3) sts.

Next row: K2, sl 1, k1, psso, k to last 4 sts, k2tog, k2.

Next row: Purl.

Repeat the last two rows 15 (16, 17, 18) more times. Sl remaining 14 (18, 20, 24) sts onto a holder.

FRONT

Work in same manner as back, repeating the last two rows until 18 (22, 24, 28) sts remain, ending with a knit row. To shape neck, p4 sts, slip center 10 (14, 16, 20) sts onto a holder, join another ball of yarn and p last 4 sts. Working in St

st on both sides at once, continue to decrease 1 st (k2tog) at each arm edge every other row twice more, and, at the same time, at each neck edge dec 1 st (k2tog) every other row twice. Bind off remaining stitch.

SLEEVES

I like to knit both sleeves at the same time on the same needle from two balls of yarn so that increases and rows are even. You may choose to knit the sleeves in the more conventional way by knitting them one at a time.

Using size 9 straight needles, cast on 32 (32, 34, 34) sts. For sizes small and medium, work in 2 × 2 rib (k2, p2 every row) for 2" (5 cm). For sizes large and extra large, work as follows for 2" (5 cm):

Row 1 (RS): *K2, p2, rep from * across row, k2.

Row 2 (WS): *P2, k2, rep from * across row, p2.

Change to size 11 straight needles and work in St st, increasing 1 st at each end of every 10th (6th, 6th, 6th) row, 5 (7, 7, 9) times. Work even on 42 (46, 48, 52) sts until piece measures 18 (18½, 19, 19½)" (46 [47, 48, 50] cm) or desired length to underarm, ending

with a purl row. At the beginning of each of the next two rows, bind off 2 (2, 3, 3) sts. Decrease in same manner as on back and front, as follows:

Next row: K2, sl 1, k1, psso, k to last 4 sts, k2tog, k2.

Next row: Purl.

Repeat these rows until 6 (8, 6, 8) sts remain. Sl remaining 6 (8, 6, 8) sts onto holder.

Finishing

Sew sleeves to back and front armholes. Sew underarm seams. Using circular needle or set of double-pointed needles, with right side facing you, pick up 56 (60, 64, 68) stitches around neck edge, including sts from holders. Work in 2 × 2 rib (k2, p2 every row) for 1" (3 cm). Bind off loosely in ribbing and sew tail of yarn into wrong side of neckline. Weave in any loose ends with yarn needle. Block if necessary to fit.

MATERIALS

The olive sweater shown here is knit in cashmere yarn leftover from a long-ago project, but a similar, if less luxurious, effect can be achieved using 8 (8, 9, 11) skeins Kraemer Yarns Mauch Chunky (100% wool; 3.5 oz [100 g]/120 yds [110 m]) in desired color

US size 9 (5.5 mm) and 11 (8 mm) straight needles; size 9 (5.5 mm) circular needles (20" [51 cm] or 24" [61 cm] length) or size 9 (5.5 mm) set of double-pointed needles for knitting crewneck or size to obtain gauge

Stitch holders

Yarn needle

Finished Dimensions

Directions are for sizes small (medium, large, extra large).

Width: (chest measurement): 32–34 (36–38, 40–42, 44–46).

Gauge: 3 sts and 4 rows = 1" (3 cm)

4" × 4" (10 × 10 cm) swatch = 12 sts and 16 rows

mittens

Knit a pair of mittens to match almost any design in this book. Here, we show
a pair of mittens with a furry textured cuff, which matches the Kwik-Knit
Shaggy Sweater featured on page 110. Use your imagination (and leftover
yarn!) to make other matching mittens based on these basic instructions.

INSTRUCTIONS FOR
MITTENS

The left- and right-hand mittens are identical to each other; simply knit two to complete the pair.

Holding MC and CC yarn together, cast on 32 sts onto four double-pointed needles (8 sts on each needle). Join stitches to work in the round, placing marker. Work in 2 × 2 rib (k2, p2 every row), holding both strands of yarn as one, for 2" (5 cm). Be sure to complete a full round (knit to the marker). Cut CC yarn, leaving a 3" (8 cm) tail. Using only MC, work decreases as follows:

First needle: K2tog, knit to end of needle.

Second needle: Knit to last 2 sts, ssk.

Third needle: K2tog, knit to end of needle.

Fourth needle: Knit to last 2 sts, ssk (28 sts).

Next row, work increase for thumb gusset as follows: K14, M1R, place marker, k1, M1L, knit to end of round. Increase 1 st before the marker and after the stitch following the marker every third row, four more times (38 sts).

Next row: K14 and place the next 10 sts on a stitch holder (these will form the thumb later). Cast on 1 new stitch to bridge the gap created by the thumb stitches and continue to knit to end of round (29 sts). Continue knitting hand portion of mitten until it reaches tip of pinky.

Next row (beginning with the needle with 8 sts on it): K2tog, knit to end of round (28 sts, 7 on each needle).

Decrease round (to shape the tip of the mitten): *K to last 2 sts on the needle, k2tog*, repeat from * to * on each needle (24 sts).

Knit one round.

Repeat decrease round (20 sts).

Knit one round.

Next three rows: Repeat decrease round (8 sts).

Pull yarn through remaining stitches and cinch to close the tip of the mitten.

TO FORM THUMB

Move first 2 sts of thumb gusset from the stitch holder onto the first double-pointed needle. Place the next 4 sts on the second needle and the final 4 sts on the third needle. With the fourth needle, pick up 2 sts from the bottom edge of the mitten body, then knit the 2 sts on the first needle. Continue to knit all stitches in a round (12 sts, 3 needles) until the thumb portion of the mitten reaches the tip of the thumb. Work decreases as follows:

Decrease round: *K2tog, k to end of needle*, repeat for each needle (9 sts).

Knit one round.

Repeat decrease round (6 sts).

Pull yarn through remaining stitches and cinch to close the tip of the mitten. Using yarn needle, weave in all loose ends to finish mitten.

MATERIALS

1 skein bulky weight yarn, Kraemer Yarns Mauch Chunky (100% wool; 3.5 oz [100 g]/120 yd [110 m]) in strawberry or desired color; 1 skein Lion Brand Yarns Fancy Fur (55% polyamide, 45% polyester; 1.75 oz [50 g]/39 yd [35 m]) in rainbow red or desired color

US size 10½" (6.5 mm) double-pointed needles

Stitch markers

Stitch holder

Yarn needle

Finished Dimensions

Sample shown is 9½" (24 cm) long × 4" (10 cm) wide. Finished length of project will vary, depending on hand size.

Gauge: approximately 3 sts and 5 rows = 1"

in stockinette stitch

4" × 4" (10 × 10 cm) swatch = 15 sts and 20 rows

Stitch Abbreviations

M1L = make one left: With left needle tip, lift strand between needles from front to back. Knit lifted loop through the back.

M1R = make one right: With left needle tip, lift strand between needles from back to front. Knit lifted loop through the front.

Pattern Graphs

To read a chart, start at the bottom row. On knit rows (right side rows), follow the chart from right to left, in the same manner that your stitches are worked from the needles. On purl rows (wrong side rows), follow the chart from left to right, as if you were reading. (For more on working with color, see page 74.)

DIAMOND TURTLENECK SWEATER, page 64

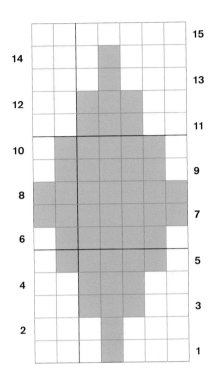

7 stitches × 15 rows

Size SMALL:
5 repeats wide × 3 repeats long

Size MEDIUM:
6 repeats wide × 4 repeats long

Size LARGE:
8 repeats wide × 7 repeats long

FAIR ISLE SWEATER, page 72

BODY CHART

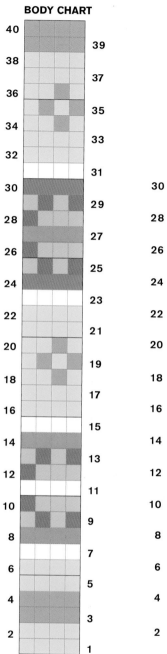

SLEEVE CHART

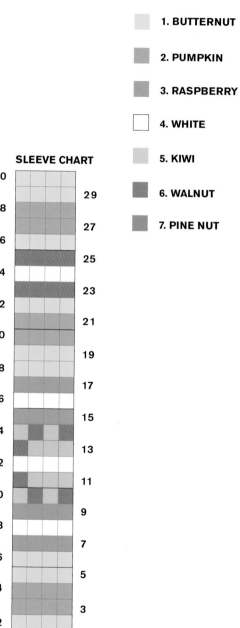

1. BUTTERNUT

2. PUMPKIN

3. RASPBERRY

4. WHITE

5. KIWI

6. WALNUT

7. PINE NUT

PERUVIAN TURTLENECK SWEATER, page 76

BODY CHART

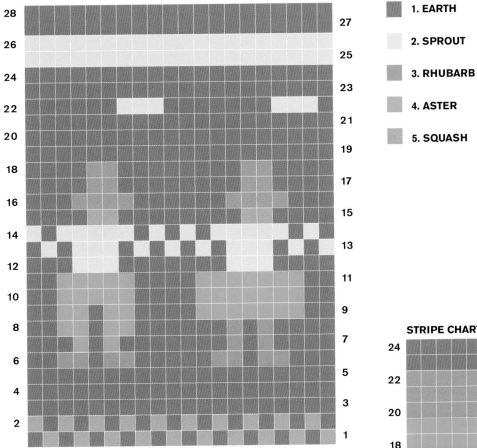

Color key:
- 1. EARTH
- 2. SPROUT
- 3. RHUBARB
- 4. ASTER
- 5. SQUASH

STRIPE CHART

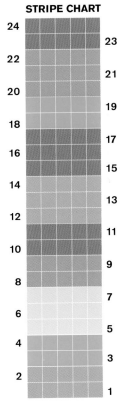

resources

A NOTE ON THE YARNS

Kraemer Yarns

Most of the yarns used in this book were provided by Kraemer Yarns, in Nazareth, Pennsylvania. The company was originally founded in 1887. Several years ago, the owners of the company, David and Victor Schmidt, opened a store to sell the mill ends of their production for the garment and home furnishings industries. Over time, the store expanded to a full selection of knitting yarns from both major companies and artisan yarn firms. It is my favorite local yarn shop.

Recently, the Schmidt brothers decided to produce a full line of yarns for the home knitter. I had the good fortune of testing these yarns, and chose to include them in the designs produced for this book. It is the first book that specifies their yarns in home knitting patterns. I thank them for providing me with the opportunity to introduce these yarns to you.

The majority of the yarns featured here are available directly from Kraemer Yarns. Several of the yarns are produced by large companies that sell their yarns to mass merchants and craft store chains, so they are readily available to most knitters. Try your local yarn stores, and if the yarns mentioned here are not available, substitute others that have the same gauge and similar properties.

Your local yarn store is a wonderful resource for alternative yarns that will produce excellent results. They can also offer the beginning knitter instruction, advice, and encouragement, as well as introducing her (or him) to a community of other people who enjoy the same diversion.

YARN RESOURCES

Adrienne Vittadini
Distributed by JCA, Inc.
35 Scales Lane
Townsend, MA 01469
USA

Anny Blatt
7796 Boardwalk
Brighton, MI 48116
USA
info@annyblattusa.com

Artful Yarns/JCA Inc.
35 Scales Lane
Townsend, MA 01469
USA
978.597.8794

Banwy Workshops
Llanfair Caereinion
Powys, Mid Wales
SY210SG
UK
44.01938.810128
Fax: 44.01938.810127
www.colinette.com

Beadworks
139 Washington Street
Norwalk, CT 06854
USA
203.852.9194
www.beadworks.com

Berroco
P. O. Box 367
14 Elmdale Road
Uxbridge, MA 01569
USA
508.278.2527
Order Line: 800.343.4948

Black Bird Buttons
by Martha Enzler
24A Main Street
Bristol, VT 05443
USA
802.453.7252

Blue Sky Alpacas
P. O. Box 367
St. Francis, MN 55070
USA

Brown Sheep
100662 County Road
Mitchell, NE 69357-9748
USA
308.635.2198
Order Line: 800.826.9136
Fax: 308.635.2143
www.brownsheep.com

Cascade Yarns
1224 Andover Park East
Tukwila, WA 98188-3905
USA

Cherry Tree Hill, Inc.
P. O. Box 659
Barton, VT 05822
USA
802.525.3311
Order Line: 800.739.7701
www.cherryyarn.com

Classic Elite
300 Jackson Street
Lowell, MA 01852-2180
USA
978.453.2837
Order Line: 800.343.0308
Fax: 978.452.3085
classicelite@aol.com

Coats & Clark
Consumer Service
P. O. Box 12229
Greenville, SC 29612-0229
USA
800.648.1479
www.coatsandclark.com

Colinette Yarns
Unique Kolours
1428 Oak Lane
Downingtown, PA 19335
USA
610.280.7720
Order Line: 800.252.3934
Fax: 610.280.7701
www.uniquekolours.com
uniquekolo@aol.com

Crystal Palace Yarns
160 23rd Street
Richmond, CA 94804
USA
www.straw.com

Dale of Norway, Inc.
N16 W23390 Stoneridge
Drive, Suite A
Waukesha, WI 53188
USA
262.544.1996
Order Line:
800.441.DALE (3253)
Fax: 262.544.1997
www.dale.no

Debbie Bliss
Distributed by
Designer Yarns
Newbridge Interbrough
Estate
Unit 8-10 Pitt Street
Keighley, West Yorkshire
BD21 4PQ
UK

Euroflax Linen Yarn
Louet Sales
808 Commerce Park Drive
Ogdensburg, NY 13669
USA
613.925.4502
Fax: 613.925.1405
www.louet.com
info@louet.com

Fiesta Yarns
4583 Corrales Road
Corrales, NM 87048
USA
505.892.5008 (wholesale)
505.792.0789 (retail)
www.fiestayarns.com
laboheme@fiestayarns.com

Filatura
Distributed by
Takhi•Stacy Charles, Inc.
77-30 80th Street
Building 36
Ridgewood, NY 11385
USA

Green Lane Mill
Holmfirth
West Yorkshire HD7 1RW
UK
01484.680050

Hand Jive Knits
977 El Camino Real #203
Burlingame, CA 94010
USA
650.685.7967
Fax: 650.685.7967
www.handjiveknits.com
darlenehayes@
handjiveknits.com
Knitting patterns and kits

Jaeger Handknits
4 Townsend West
Unit 8
Nashua, NH 03063
USA

Karabella Yarns
1201 Broadway
Suite 311
New York, NY 10001
USA
212.684.2665
arthurkarapetyan@aol.com

KnitKit
92498 Airport Road
Sixes, OR 97476
USA
541.348.2580
www.knitkit.com
janet@knitkit.com
*Knitting patterns with a specialty
in knitted bags designed by
Janet Scanlon*

Knitting Fever, Inc.
and Euro Yarns
35 Debevoise Avenue
Roosevelt, NY 11575
USA
516.546.3600
Fax: 516.546.6871
www.knittingfever.com
webmaster@
knittingfever.com
*Distributor of Sirdar, Noro,
Katia, Gedifra, Knitting Fever,
Debbie Bliss, On Line, Euro
Yarns, Mondial, Jo Sharp, and
Schachenmayr yarns*

Koigu Wool Designs
RR #1
Williamsford, ON NCH 2VO
Canada

Kraemer Yarns
240 South Main Street
Nazareth, PA 18064
USA
800.759.5601
610.759.4030
Fax: 610.759.4157
www.KraemerYarns.com

La Lana Wools
136 Paseo Norte
Taos, NM 87571
USA
505.758.9631
Order Line: 888.377.9631
www.lalanawools.com
lalana@lalanawools.com

Lion Brand Yarns
34 West 15th Street
New York, NY 10011
USA
212.243.8995
Order Line: 800.795.LION
Fax: 212.627.8154
www.lionbrand.com

Manos del Uruguay
Design Source (distributor)
P. O. Box 770
Medford, MA 02155
USA
781.438.6279
Order Line: 888.566.9970
shangold@aol.com

Mission Falls
Unique Kolours
1428 Oak Lane
Downingtown, PA 19335
USA
610.280.7720
Order Line: 800.252.3934
Fax: 610.280.7701
www.uniquekolours.com
uniquekolo@aol.com

in Canada:
P. O. Box 224
Consecon, Ontario K0K 1T0
Canada
613.392.4131
Fax: 613.392.1269
www.missionfalls.com

Mountain Colors
P. O. Box 156
Corvallis, MT 59828
USA

studio address:
4072 Eastside Highway
Stevensville, MT 59870
USA
Fax: 406.777.7313
www.mountaincolors.com
info@mountaincolors.com

My Yarn Shop
264B South Broadway
Coos Bay, OR 97420
USA
541.266.8230
Order Line: 888.664.9276
www.myyarnshop.com
knitting@myyarnshop.com

Patons
P. O. Box 40
Listowel, ON N4W 3H3
Canada
www.patonsyarns.com

Plymouth Yarn
P. O. Box 28
Bristol, PA 19007
USA
www.plymouthyarn.com

Reynolds/JCA, Inc.
35 Scales Lane
Townsend, MA
01469-1094
USA
978.597.8794

Rowan Yarns
4 Townsend West
Unit 8
Nashua, NH 03063
USA

in the UK:
Green Lane Mill
Holmfirth
West Yorkshire HD7 1RW
UK
01484.681881

S. R. Kertzer, Ltd.
105A Winges Road
Woodbridge, ON L4L 6C2
Canada
800.263.2354
www.kertzer.com

Tahki•Stacy Charles, Inc.
8000 Cooper Avenue,
Building 1
Glendale, NY 11385
USA
718.326.4433
www.tahkistacycharles.com
info@tahkistacycharles.com

Tangled Yarns
519 Main Street
Bethlehem, PA 18018
USA
610.867.0318

Skacel Collection
P. O. Box 88110
Seattle, WA 98138-2110
USA
800.255.1278

Trendsetter Yarns
16742 Stagg, #104
Van Nuys, CA 91406
USA
818.780.5497
Order Line: 800.446.2425
trndstr@aol.com

Tucker Yarn
950 Hamilton Street
Allentown, PA 18101
USA
610.434.1846
Fax: 610.433.3835
caston@tuckeryarn.com
www.tuckeryarn.com

contributors

The wonderful photographs in this book were taken by Rob Upton of Rob Upton Photography, 3245 Darien Road, Bethlehem, PA 18020, 610.814.0611. photobyrob@rcn.com

The mitten photograph on page 116 was taken by Allan Penn of Allan Penn Photography, 33 Commercial Street, Gloucester, MA 01930.

All of the projects were designed by the author, except for the Mittens (page 116), which were designed by Rochelle Bourgault of Rockport Publishers.

All the project samples in the book were knit by the author, except for the Contrast Turtleneck Sweater (page 96) and the Mittens (page 116), which were knit by Rochelle Bourgault of Rockport Publishers.

acknowledgments

This book could not have been written without the help of some very special individuals. I would like to thank my editor, Delilah Smittle; publisher, Winnie Prentiss; project manager, Rochelle Bourgault; and the rest of the staff at Rockport Publishers, who participated in the successful creation of this book. I also want to thank Ellen Phillips, who introduced me to the Rockport team. My photographer, Rob Upton, made the photo shoots a delight. Sue Repash, of A.B.E. Veterinary Hospital in Allentown, Pennsylvania, was kind to function as my "talent agent." I must also thank my veterinarian, Karen Hess, of Walbert Animal Hospital in Allentown, Pennsylvania, for her encouragement and support.

A tremendous thank-you to all the "pet parents" who made the time to come to the photo shoots, and who functioned as "animal wranglers." I could not have done it without you! And a big hug to all of my "supermodels"—you are the best!

Mark and Peggy Buckley and Mei-Mei
Mary Cornell and Lea
Bill Cosgrove and Zeke and Eddie
Jan Esposito and Abbey and Micky
Chrissy Kacsur and Carter
Donna Kowalskie and Nicki
Carol Lovgren and Kumi
Craig Lovgren and Charlotte
Carol Mickey and Chloe
Kacee Mickey and Winston
Lari Perovich and Bear
Stephanie Pickel and Jasper

Sue Repash and Friday, Ivan the Terrier, Tazzie, and Sadie B.
Kimberly Rohrbach and Pogo
Lori Salivonchik and Riley
Victor Schmidt and Aggie, Mocha, and Kendall
Amanda Hudock Staver and Maddie and Lira
Barbara Toczek and Boka, Belitta, Bambam, Baja, and Besa
Rob Upton and Cuddles
Bob Wood and Kelly

I recognize the help provided by my favorite local knitting store, Kraemer Yarns of Nazareth, Pennsylvania. David and Victor Schmidt, the proprietors of the yarn mill and shop, were kind enough to supply me with their new line of yarns. I also want to thank Eileen Novak and Jo Anne Turcotte, the managers of the store, who thought to introduce me to the Schmidt brothers. This book would not be the same without all of your help.

Finally, I would be remiss if I did not express my deep gratitude to my family and friends. You are my lifeline. Each one of you knows how much I cherish you. You've always been here for me, and I hope that I reciprocate your affection and support in some small measure:

Bob Wood
Irwin Hochberg
Trudy Berhang
Bernard Rosenthal
Malvina and Joseph Farkas
Lou Solomon
Holly Rosenthal
Joelle, Bradley, and Howard Bernstein
Carol, Seth, Lindy, Hayleigh, Steven, Gail, Alex, Rachel, and Daniel Hochberg
Anya, Albert, and Olivia Salama
Carl D'Aquino
José Valdes-Fauli
Shed Boren
Stephanie Freed
Marina Kats

Jeanne Mathews
Gail Solomon
Joyce Heverley
Thierry Soursac
Steve Brown
Steven Saide
Jack Hruska
Siggy Zises
Nancy, Jay, and Merryl Zises
Lynn, Doug, Isabelle, and Mack Krugman
Dana, Joshua, and Sara Meltzer
Alison Lehrer
Damien Wood
Kelly McFadden
Jonas Wood and Jen Sayuk
Bargie Cat and Kelly

about the author

Ilene Rosenthal Hochberg is an internationally bestselling author whose parody books have made millions of people laugh over the absurdities of life. Her examination of the anthropomorphism of animals (treating our pets as people) has been met with great acclaim. Her books *Dogue, Catmopolitan, Vanity Fur, Forbabes, Good Mousekeeping,* and *Who Stole My Cheese?!!!* are perennial favorites, and have been featured in various media including CNN, *Good Morning Everywhere,* PBS, *Newsweek, Forbes, The Wall Street Journal, Vanity Fair, Good Housekeeping, Cosmopolitan, Advertising Age,* and the *New York Times* best-seller list.

Ms. Hochberg's education includes a BS in Design and Environmental Analysis from Cornell University. She is a member of Mensa, has been an instructor at the Parsons School of Design, is a designer of functional fashions for pets, holds a black belt in shopping, and is a confirmed knitter. In other words, she is the ideal person to have written this book.